A
PRACTICAL
COMPANION
TO
ETHICS

A

PRACTICAL

COMPANION

TO

ETHICS

FOURTH EDITION

Anthony Weston
Elon University

New York   Oxford
OXFORD UNIVERSITY PRESS
2011

OXFORD
UNIVERSITY PRESS

Oxford University Press, Inc., publishes works that further
Oxford University's objective of excellence
in research, scholarship, and education.

Oxford New York
Auckland Cape Town Dar es Salaam Hong Kong Karachi
Kuala Lumpur Madrid Melbourne Mexico City Nairobi
New Delhi Shanghai Taipei Toronto

With offices in
Argentina Austria Brazil Chile Czech Republic France Greece
Guatemala Hungary Italy Japan Poland Portugal Singapore
South Korea Switzerland Thailand Turkey Ukraine Vietnam

Published by Oxford University Press, Inc.
198 Madison Avenue, New York, New York 10016
www.oup.com

Oxford is a registered trademark of Oxford University Press.

Library of Congress Cataloging-in-Publication Data

Weston, Anthony, 1954–
A practical companion to ethics / Anthony Weston.—4th ed.
p. cm.
Includes bibliographical references.
ISBN 978-0-19-973058-2
1. Ethics. I. Title.
BJ1025.W43 2010
170—dc22
2010024790

Printing number: 11

Printed in the United States of America
on acid-free paper

CONTENTS

PREFACE

Ethics is regularly in the news. Sometimes we hear of extraordinary acts of devotion or courage. More often we hear of moral lapses, from personal tragedies to misdeeds that damage entire communities. We have gotten used to commenting on the ethical news almost like we comment on the weather. But ethics actually needs much more systematic attention.

Our ethical debates seem to be reducing to louder and longer fights. We get stuck in conflicts or "dilemmas" and find ourselves going nowhere, or around the same old circles too many times. Changing anything seems to be out of the question, since open-minded thinking about values is so often pictured as morally weak or indecisive. And to top it off, we readily get discouraged about making any real ethical difference.

Yet there is hope. For you might notice something else about these types of problems. They all involve *learnable skills*. And therefore there is no reason why we cannot foster far more effective and constructive ways of approaching ethical issues and embrace far higher hopes for ourselves and each other as potential ethical change-makers.

Open and inquiring minds can be *developed*. The ability and eagerness to think critically and persistently about values and issues can be deepened. So, too, can the simple courage to think for yourself. It may even be a source of inspiration to realize that there is more to ethics than just following some pre-given set of rules. Certainly it may open up entirely different and more productive approaches to ethical disagreements.

We can think more *systematically* about values with some knowledge of the traditional reference-points in philosophical ethics. Ethical theories can help us clarify values and give some shape to ethical conflicts.

We can think more *constructively* about values by looking at their tensions not as head-on clashes but as a sign—in fact, as a welcome reminder—that our values are complex and varied. Mightn't a more deft and far-sighted practice actually make use of that complexity and variety to find more inclusive ways forward?

We can think more *creatively* about values with a few simple skills that enable us to open up unexpected space and new options in what seem to be "stuck" moral problems or dilemmas. Some encouragement and practical advice can help us step up to making real ethical change in our own lives and the world as well.

The aim of this book is to help you advance and expand some of these basic ethical attitudes and skills. It will not make you an ethical sage or an expert—only a lot more experience and maturity can do that. But it can, at least, bring certain key attitudes and skills into the spotlight and give you a sense of how much difference even some small improvements in those attitudes and skills can make. This book places ethics against a larger practical and philosophical background, and invites you to take the next few steps down the road.

In a college setting, this book is designed to enrich the usual first presentation of ethics in practical fields like journalism, nursing, or business, and at the same time to complement the usual first presentation of ethics proper in the philosophy curriculum. Academic philosophy can sometimes become preoccupied with certain intellectual challenges unique to ethics, and consequently may slight the broader practical skills essential in ethics but not necessarily unique to it. Part of the aim of this book is to rejoin ethics to larger life skills—to put ethics into its rightful place. It invites the practical reader into more fully engaged and energetic philosophical thinking at the same time that it invites the philosophical reader into a more fully engaged and energetic practice.

For the criticism and advice that helped shape this fourth edition of *A Practical Companion to Ethics*, I am grateful to many students and colleagues, as well as close readings by the publisher's reviewers: Nancy Billias at Saint Joseph College, Jurgis Brakas at Marist College, Daniel Campana at University of La Verne, Peter Dalton at Florida State University, Robert Jensen at the University of Texas, and Brad Musil at the University of Kansas, as well as several anonymous readers. The results are more significant changes in this edition than between previous editions. Overall, the level of the writing has edged up somewhat. I have tried to give the exercises—the "For Practice" sections—a sharper assignment-oriented focus, as many users requested. This edition offers an entirely new chapter on ethical theories, making it farther-reaching for ethics-related courses where it might be the only philosophical text, and likewise a more useful first sketch of practical ethics, broadly conceived, within philosophy. Chapters 4 and 5, on how to deal with conflicts of values and on creative problem-solving in ethics, are greatly revised and somewhat expanded as well. A new final chapter, "Making a Difference," speaks to many teachers' wish to bring ethics more directly into practice. In place of previous editions' appendix, this chapter offers a box on "Writing to Make a Difference," reflecting a shift in my own teaching away from using papers as primarily an academic exercise and toward embedding writing into the service and change work of the course.

Many changes. At the same time, I have tried to keep this book true to its chief aim from the very first edition: to be a modest, companionate, practical, and optimistic supplement to the more traditional material in ethics courses. Of course it still can offer only the barest sketch of a very complex topic. For a much fuller treatment of all of this book's themes, readers may wish to follow up with my full-scale textbook *A 21st Century Ethical Toolbox* (second edition, New York/Oxford: Oxford University Press, 2008; third edition forthcoming). *Toolbox* also includes two extensive appendices dealing with some of the methodological issues raised by a resolutely practical approach to ethics and offering detailed suggestions for teaching this material as well.

As always, I would be honored to hear from students and teachers on any of this book's themes—and, especially, to hear how you have made good use of these philosophical skills in ethics to make a difference in the world.

Anthony Weston
weston@elon.edu

A
PRACTICAL
COMPANION
TO
ETHICS

1

GETTING STARTED

~

First of all, ethics invites and provokes us to *think*. Ethics is a learning experience. And so, as with any learning experience, you must bring your mind, keep it open, and keep it active.

WHO NEEDS ETHICS?

Take the question of passion—of feeling. Feeling is essential, for sure. A life without love, excitement, and even pain is no life at all. Ethics itself draws on the passions: the passions to make a difference, to see more deeply, to act more honorably, to do the right thing.

Sometimes, though, we are tempted to stop as soon as we've started, as if ethical passion were enough all by itself. People who feel very strongly about certain ethical issues sometimes take the strength of their feelings to settle ethical questions without any further consideration at all. Conversely, we often get a hint (or more than a hint) that a person who has mixed or uncertain moral feelings is somehow a less moral person—as if, again, the most ethical person must be the one with the strongest and clearest ethical feelings. Could feelings really be *it?*

In fact, there is more to the story. Feelings may be the beginning but cannot be the end. The key thing is this: *our passions themselves may need critical direction or redirection*—even though the need for rethinking our passions may be hard to accept when we are in the grips of them. It is possible to be passionate about the wrong things. All kinds of morally bad things—slavery, for instance—have had heartfelt and even courageous defenders. All the same, they were wrong, and their feelings had to change. Ethics comes up precisely in the *questioning.*

A milder example is prejudice. To be prejudiced is to have a negative feeling about someone who is of a different ethnicity or gender or age or social class (or ...) from yourself. If ethics were chiefly a matter of feelings, then there would be nothing to say against such prejudices. It would be perfectly moral to discriminate against people you do not like. As you know very well, though, ethics asks more than this. *Prejudice* literally means "prejudgment": it is a way of not really paying attention. But we *need* to pay attention. We need to ask why we feel as we do, whether our beliefs and feelings are true or fair, how *we* would feel in the other person's shoes. In short, we need to ask whether our feelings are *justified*—and, when not, what might be alternative and more justified feelings.

Ethics asks us, in general, to live mindfully—to think through how we act and even how we feel. It may ask us to take the harder and more unsettling path, to make things more complex and uncertain rather than simpler. Patience is often essential too. Where things are really unclear, feelings may even have to wait. Premature clarity is worse than confusion. We may have to live with some issues for a long time before we can decide how we *ought* to feel about them. That's a moral question!

Feelings may also easily be manipulated. We may be swayed by "loaded language"—language that plays on our emotional reactions. Define *abortion* as "baby killing" and you create a negative feeling that closes the case against abortion before it can even be opened. But "fetuses" are not "babies" (look up the words). On the other hand, if you describe abortion as no more than minor surgery, you suggest that it is unintrusive and even healthy. Either way, we are led into a prepackaged emotional commitment without carefully thinking it through.

Mindful thinking, by contrast, is more open-ended. It is in this spirit that ethics invites us to take up controversial issues of the day, like abortion or professional ethics or the status of other animals. We do care for other animals, for instance. But we also use many of them for food, clothes, chemical tests, and even as objects of sport. Should all of this stop? No? Well, should *any* of it stop? Probably. So what kinds of use of other animals should stop and what kinds should not? Why? How do you decide?

These questions cannot be adequately answered by just consulting our feelings. There are too many different possibilities, too many different "uses," and too many different opinions and prejudices (on all sides) that need to be carefully sorted out. Again, it takes some time and care.

It may also require some degree of compromise—or some unexpected alternative approach. This book will suggest that much more intelligent and creative thinking is possible about this and many other ethical issues. The key word is *thinking*. That's the challenge of ethics!

WHAT IS ETHICS?

What is ethics? Philosophers and dictionaries often say something like this: ethics is *the study of moral values*; it is *reflection on how best to understand moral values and to clarify, prioritize, and practice them.*

This definition in turn depends on several others. What are "values," for one thing? In this book, by "values" I will mean *those things we care about; those things that matter to us; those goals or ideals to which we aspire and by which measure ourselves and others and our society.*

When we speak of "moral" values, we are concerned with a specific kind of values: *those values that give voice to the needs and legitimate expectations of others as well as ourselves.* "Legitimate expectations" may be of many sorts: we rightly expect to be treated with respect, for instance, and with honesty and care. Exactly what expectations are legitimate, of course, is itself an ethical question.

Although we often use the terms "ethics" and "morals" interchangeably, it is helpful to distinguish the moral values we happen to hold from the deliberate process of thinking them through, criticizing and revising them. The term "ethics" has more of a critical, self-conscious edge. Again: ethics asks us to go beyond *living out* our values to *thinking them through.*

THE DOGMATIST AND THE RATIONALIZER

There are a variety of all-too-ready counterfeits for real ethical thinking. Looked at in the clear light of day, these are really forms of *avoiding* ethical thinking. Often, though, they cleverly disguise themselves as forms of thinking, too. We need to guard ourselves against them.

Why Listen?

We all know the kind of people who are so committed to their moral beliefs that they cannot see any other side, no matter how many facts or further considerations come along. This can *look* like thinking—after all, they may be giving reasons and justifications and making arguments, even if rather repetitive and loud ones—but in fact it is dogmatism. They may appear to listen, but they *will not* change their minds. Name "their" issue (or perhaps *any* issue) and they know the answer already.

To be very clear: being committed to a certain set of values—living up to them, or trying to, and sticking up for them when we can—is a fine thing. And there are certain basic moral values to which we are and *should be* deeply and unshakably committed. The problem is that dogmatists go much further. They make no distinction between the basic "givens" of our moral life and everyday moral opinions that are not at all so clear-cut. Every one of their moral judgments, to them, has the same status as the Ten Commandments.

Dogmatists tend to disagree about the actual issues—which would be amusing if it were not so common, since the whole point is supposed to be that the Truth is so simple and obvious that it needs only mentioning to be instantly decisive. Dogmatists do agree, though, that careful and open-ended thinking about moral issues is not necessary. After all, if you already know the answer, there is no need to actually think about it, is there? If you need to argue for your position, you admit that it needs defending, which is to say that people can legitimately have doubts. But that cannot be true: you already know that your position is the only right one. Therefore, any reasoned argument for your position is unnecessary. And any reasoned argument against your position is obviously absurd. So, why listen?

Ethics, once again, paints a different picture. Despite the stereotypes, the point of ethics is generally not to moralize or to dictate what is to be done. The real point of ethics is to offer some tools, and some possible directions, for thinking about difficult matters, recognizing from the start—as the very *rationale* for ethics, in fact—that the world is seldom so simple or clear-cut. Struggle and uncertainty are part of ethics, as they are part of life.

After all, ethics by its very nature concerns some of the hardest and most complex of our choices. Here, surely, most of the time at least, we need to listen, to keep at least a *somewhat* open mind. Otherwise doggedness is likely to blind us, to make us insensitive and unresponsive. Even a few new facts might change everything. We do not want to end up like the person Mark Twain once described as "so full of what's right that he cannot see what's good." Crack the door open a little. Turn on some lights.

One practical tool for avoiding dogmatism is to avoid casting ethical issues or positions in loaded and categorical terms. Start by opening up your very language. Instead of categorical statements of dogmatic opinions, for example with bumper sticker–style slogans ("Meat is murder," "God is pro-life," etc.), try to speak in a way that is less categorical and final. No reasonable moral positions can be shoehorned into a bumper sticker or slogan, clever as it might be—and besides, this way of putting things polarizes views and makes the other side seem just stupid and misled. Do not call names either ("You animal-rights fanatics..."; "You Bible-thumpers..."). Avoid the easy labels ("liberal," "right-wing," ...).

Speaking in a more open-ended way may help you begin to think in a more open-ended way, too. At the very least it will open up more constructive conversations! Typically one dogmatic statement just provokes an equal and opposite dogmatic statement. Speak differently, and not only your mind but also your discussions may unfold very differently, and much more constructively, too.

Offhand Self-justification

Another kind of counterfeit thinking actually does offer reasons but without any real critical thinking or engagement. Let us call it "offhand self-justification."

Suppose I offer some view in a moral discussion. Someone challenges me. My natural first reaction is to defend whatever it was I just said—even (maybe especially) if the challenge is exactly on target. It is a kind of automatic excuse-making or defensiveness. I may not even get to the point of asking if the challenge actually is on target. Indeed, that's the idea. I'd rather not. Self-defense is all that counts. I try to paper over my uncertainties (or insecurities, or half-knowledge, or wishful thinking) by grabbing for some excuse—and any excuse will do. "It is OK to cheat the telephone company, because ... because, well, everyone else does it, too... because the telephone company cheats *you* ... because ... ."

Asked for your reasons, you should give them. There is nothing wrong with trying to explain and defend yourself. The problem lies with the offhand or robotic spirit (or, more accurately, spiritlessness) of this kind of self-defense. "Rationalization" actually becomes an excuse for not really thinking at all.

> S: Of course the death penalty deters murders. It is a proven fact that murder rates are lower in states with the death penalty.
>
> A: I'm not so sure about that. My understanding is that most states with the death penalty have *higher* murder rates.
>
> S: Well, you can prove anything with numbers.

At first glance, S's reply may seem reasonable enough. It may be true that "numbers" can (seem to) support a variety of different and even opposite positions. But surely this calls for *more* care and caution in using them, not less—certainly not simply tossing a statistical claim into an argument and then abandoning it the moment there is any critical headwind. S initially appeals to "numbers"—comparative murder rates—to support her position. Challenged, she does not reconsider her position or explore other possibilities. She just dismisses any studies that disagree with what she believes—and in the process manages to dismiss the very "numbers" she herself just cited.

But she does not even notice. It's all offhand. You can tell that in the next discussion she will be right back citing the same "proven fact" again. It seems clear that she was not offering an informed or serious argument in the first place.

There are no sure-fire ways to avoid offhand self-justification. It takes a kind of self-confidence, honesty, and maturity that develop slowly, and even then we seldom escape the temptation entirely. Sometimes it is hard even to recognize an offhand self-justification when it is right in front of our eyes. Yet there are some useful strategies for overcoming the urge.

Remind yourself how self-defeating it is. Making excuses only allows us to go on with some questionable behavior until we get into even worse trouble. It may even be worse than merely hanging onto one unintelligent opinion. When we rationalize, we usually saddle ourselves with *more and more* unsupportable opinions—new ones invented, off the top of the head, to patch up the holes in the old ones. But the new ones are likely to be full of holes too. Do not even start down that path.

Watch yourself. Step a little more slowly the next time you find yourself casting about for some excuse to put questions to rest. Ask instead whether you really are justified in the first place.

Watch for that tell-tale anger or irritation at being challenged. We often find ourselves becoming irritated or angry when our especially precious excuses are too persistently or effectively challenged by someone else. But, of course, we get angry at the person challenging us, rather than considering that it might really be our fault for offering an offhand excuse in the first place. Anger at someone else keeps us from having to be angry at ourselves. It is wiser to take the irritation as a warning sign.

Avoid the automatic counterattack. Again, watch yourself. Listening to others argue, are you trying to understand, or just waiting for them to stop so that you can give your comeback? Are you trying to learn or just to win? Watch your voice tone: are you conveying ridicule, irritation? Better to back off and acknowledge that maybe, just maybe, surprisingly enough, you do not possess the complete and final Truth on this question. Couldn't there be a little more to learn?

ETHICS AND DIVERSITY

Another kind of ethics-avoidance is often called "relativism"—a tricky but intriguing topic.

Moral values certainly vary. Maybe I think that speeding is morally acceptable, but you do not. Some societies tolerate homeless populations running into the millions; other societies find it shameful to allow even one person to sleep in the streets. Some cultures condemn sex between unmarried young people; others do not care or even encourage it.

Recognizing differences like these can lead us to a useful humility. It helps open our minds a little. And it can give us some space, sometimes, to try to figure things out for ourselves. What is right for you may *not* always be right for me.

It is tempting, though, to go much further. From our differences about moral values, some people conclude that there is no way, or no need, to think carefully or critically about values at all. "It is all relative," people say. Mind your own business. Maybe any moral opinion is really as good as the next.

"Relativism" is therefore often considered a threat or challenge to mindfulness in ethics. Is it really?

Diversity and Common Values

Maybe not. For one thing, the diversity of values is probably overrated. Sometimes values appear to vary just because we have different beliefs about the facts. Maybe I am not bothered by speeding because I think it is perfectly safe, whereas you do not. Still, we both value safety in the same way. That is the basic value involved—and one that, in this case, does not vary.

How diverse are basic values? It is an open question. Some philosophers claim that ethics itself is framed by agreements about certain *very* basic values: that we should not cause pain to innocent others, for example, or to mislead others for your own ends. Every society must promote a certain degree of respect for others' lives, and a certain degree of transparency in social and economic relations, if it is to function at all. Other basic values may still be "relative," though, such as the values attached to sex roles—one example of a kind of value that seems to vary a great deal more between cultures. The relativity of values, then, may be somewhat partial—and as the values involved become more basic and more essential, they may converge as well.

A more practical limit to relativism is that we mostly deal with people who share many of our values—where critical moral thinking has a natural place to start. Maybe in the end it is really true that you and I cannot argue with, say, cannibals about the ethics of cannibalism. Maybe. But how often do you argue with cannibals? I have never argued with a cannibal, not even once, but I argue constantly with my own children, whose moral habits, as well as eating habits, need some improvement. And I *can* argue with them—they are growing into *our* culture and have some learning to do. Here, where most of our moral argument actually takes place, there is a solid basis for going on together.

Diversity and Critical Thinking

Now consider those cases where values really do differ, even at the basic level. It still does not follow that our brains can be left to slip into idle. For one thing, differences between our own and others' values are no reason that we should not think more critically about our own. There is plenty to learn right there. However differently you and your friends and family may think about the ethics of eating animals, for example, *you* may still end up changing your diet or other practices once you think the question through for yourself.

Actually, the same goes for our arguments or discussions with others. People disagree about all kinds of things—Is there life on Mars? Did the butler do it?—but we do not suppose these other disagreements cannot be addressed or pursued intelligently. In fact, in these other cases, disagreements usually provoke us to *more* critical thinking. So why not in ethics, too? The fact that some people are racists, for example, does not prove that racism is only wrong "for us." More likely it proves that people have some learning to do.

Thus, although relativism may appear to be the very model of open-mindedness, it actually can have just the opposite effect. It can begin to *close* our minds instead.

> U: I support the death penalty. I believe that it saves lives because it makes murderers think twice before killing someone. As the Bible says, "An eye for an eye, a tooth for a tooth."
>
> V: I don't agree.
>
> U: Why?
>
> V: I just don't. That's my opinion and it is as good as yours!

That may be a little blatant, but you get the idea. Here relativism slides immediately into offhand self-justification. V treats it like a magic key to escape any kind of thinking whatsoever. She cannot even be bothered to offer any reasons, let alone engage U's.

In fact, all opinions on this and most moral subjects require further thinking. Are U's reasons good ones? What values stand on the other side? What could be V's reasons *against* the death penalty? Is the death penalty really a deterrent? Doesn't the Bible also tell us not to kill? In short: whether values are "relative" or not, there is no way out of some good hard thinking.

Diversity as the Occasion for Ethics

Sometimes, in fact, it is the very diversity of values that creates the *need* for ethics. Certain decisions shape our lives together, and so affect all of us. If the air is polluted, for example, it does not merely affect the polluters or people who think pollution is morally unproblematic. All of us have to breathe it. If our country joins a war effort or bans genetically modified foods or legalizes assisted suicide, all of us are to some degree affected.

> D: I oppose abortion.
> E: Why don't you just mind your own business? Like the slogan says, if you're against abortion, then don't have one!

But there is more to it than this. If some of us practice abortion and some do not, the result is a society in which abortion is practiced. The rest of us in the society have to stand for it, at least insofar as we have to stand aside. In such matters, we cannot act as though everyone can simply do as they please without anyone else being affected.

The relativist's stock phrase "Mind your own business" is therefore an antisocial response as well. It not only avoids thinking on the relativist's part: it also refuses to acknowledge that on issues like these we still need to work out some intelligent and mutually respectful way of going on together. These matters—certain basic moral issues—are not just "your own" but *everyone's* business.

Some philosophers argue, in fact, that this is the very point of ethics: to help us arrive at certain standards that we all are to live by when all of us are affected by each other's behavior. Some even use this point to build a theory of ethics. In their view, ethics is precisely *for* those cases where "Mind your own business!" does not work as an approach to a problem. Instead, we need to work things out together—however much we may differ. We still need to stay in touch, keep thinking, and keep talking. *That* is nothing less than ethics in practice.

ETHICS AS A LEARNING EXPERIENCE

Ethical thinking is part of our calling as responsible adults and members of our moral communities. It can also be an unmatched learning experience—an occasion for deep and continuing personal, intellectual, and moral growth. It can be a vital and fascinating way to enrich our thinking, to make our moral and cultural traditions more truly our own, and in the end to help sustain or reshape them as well. Here are some ways to embrace ethics in the spirit of learning.

Welcome Challenges

We grow the most when responding to challenges: engaging very different views, discovering that issues are more complex (or just plain different) than we thought, or finding ways to act effectively and responsibly in a changing world. In the name of growth, welcome challenges like these.

In fact, go further: seek them out. Naturally enough we gravitate toward people who mostly agree with us. When we want news, we tend to seek out sources that reinforce what we already think, especially as tailored online news and opinion services proliferate. But do you really want to arrange your whole world so you can live comfortably within the opinions you already have? Real learning and growth invite us to head in the other direction. Seek out some people and news sources with which you do *not* agree. Aim to live a little *less* comfortably—outside the tight circle of "group-think." Let challenges stretch your mind even when you continue to disagree. They will certainly make you think!

Pursue the Facts

Even a few simple facts can change everything. So seek them out, honestly and persistently. Do children raised by gay couples grow up sexually confused (more than the average adolescent)? Who actually is on welfare? How are the animals that we eat actually treated? What have been the results in countries where assisted suicide (or marijuana use, or living together without marriage...) is legal and accepted?

All of these questions are primarily factual. Actual evidence is available, although it can be ambiguous at times. No more flying by stereotypes! People on all sides of these moral debates will probably be surprised, and stimulated, by the answers. You can find them – but it takes looking.

Broaden Your Experience

Seek out experiences that will ground you in the real worlds of others. Do not presume to judge homeless people or CEOs or teenagers or lesbians or soldiers or "today's youth" (or foreigners, cops, striking workers, handicapped children, radicals, poor people, rich people, the depressed, activists from all ends of the spectrum...) until you actually know a few. Or more than a few. Or maybe just quit trying to sort everyone or everything into fixed moral categories in the first place. Travel to a few foreign countries, avoid the "tourist bubble," and, again, just pay attention. Welcome your new *mental* space.

Expect Depth

Ethical issues are usually complicated. There is always more to know about them: about the relevant values, about the background facts, the history of the issue, and what factors and forces lie behind it. Did you know that the abortion issue did not really come up in America until the 1960s—and that conservatives and liberals then favored more or less the opposite policies that they advocate now? (How could that be?) Why are some corporations vastly ahead of others in formulating (and following) codes of business ethics? How is "restorative justice"—reconciliation rather than retribution—possible, especially when crimes of extreme violence have been committed? Always be willing to explore and learn more.

Welcome Change

Deeper and more thoughtful ethical experience will change you. You go to work and begin to wonder about how to make your company's effects on the community or the land more positive. You have a friend or a family member who has an accident or a challenged child, and suddenly you have both more sympathy for others and more passion for the moment. Our culture is shifting, too: to the Fourth of July's celebration of independence, for example, we are now adding Earth Day's celebration of *inter*dependence—the insistence that we are deeply dependent on the rest of the biosphere for our health, wealth, and very survival and that it might therefore be a good idea to treat nature with more respect. Even something as obvious as recycling did not cross people's minds for generations, but it will surely be basic to any sustainable ethic in the future. What's next?

FOR PRACTICE

Review

Summarize and review the main points of this chapter. What *is* ethics, anyway? Why does it require thinking, especially when thinking is hard and often uncomfortable and we already are pretty sure how we feel about the issues?

What's wrong with "offhand self-justification"? What are some concrete strategies for resisting dogmatism? Why does the text accuse moral relativists of being antisocial? And what are some good ways to keep alive the spirit of ethics as a learning experience?

Self-reflection

We have noted some of the ways in which people close their minds, often without even noticing or admitting what is happening. Do you? (Probably! Anyway, I know I do ... .) If so, when? When do you get dogmatic? About certain issues more than others? Which ones? When do you tend to rationalize? When do you get defensive? What kinds of values or moral beliefs do you have trouble understanding? Why?

Give yourself some credit, too. What are you good at hearing? On what topics are you truly open-minded? And why is this?

Consider what events in your life you now see as ethical learning experiences. What did you learn? How about in other people's lives—people you admire, for example? Look for biographies or autobiographies of notably ethical people (and maybe also some notably unethical people) and pay attention to the ways in which they learned and changed (or did not)—what made moral learning and change possible for them. Or interview your parents, older friends, leaders, and others, asking questions like: What have been major ethical changes in your life? Why did those changes happen? Were they hard? Why? How do you feel about them now that you look back at them? What advice do you have for younger people looking ahead to such changes in their own lives?

Exploring Challenging Views

Pick a moral position that you find especially hard to take seriously. As an exercise in sustained ethical thinking and learning, try to take it seriously.

First, state the position in as neutral a way as possible. Do not be effusive or overstated—just try to state the position in a reasonable way, like you would state it if it were your own. You may have to do some research to get it right. In class, ask a classmate who holds that position to help you out.

Now explore the best reasons that might be advanced to support this view. Avoid the stereotypical arguments (often just slogans) that anyone can rattle off without thinking. Actually spell the arguments out carefully. What are the most plausible reasons according to you—the reasons that would persuade you if any reasons could? (That is, try to do more than just report on the position—try to get inside it more fully.)

You do not have to end up agreeing with this position—after all, you picked it because you not only disagree with it but find it hard even to take seriously. The point is to try to understand it, and in general to try to get a little distance from your own reactions: to create a little more space for listening and learning.

A Dialogue

The kinds of ethics-avoidance discussed in this chapter are partly conversational or argumentative moves: that is, they occur in the back-and-forth of conversation or argument. Often they are subtle, too—part of the aim, after all, is to disguise them from others and, often, even from ourselves.

Read the following exchange (more than once) and consider where—and why—you think that minds are closed or closing. Then try rewriting the exchange to illustrate a little more thoughtfulness. (And notice, as you rework it, that there are quite a lot of potentially fertile ideas here if you give them a less reactive and judgmental kind of attention.)

F: Eating meat is natural! People have always done it. I like the bumper-sticker that goes: I LOVE ANIMALS— THEY TASTE GOOD!

H: Bumper-sticker ethics, why didn't I think of that?

F: Come on, how can you argue with nature?

G: Yeah, I suppose people have always lined up at McDonald's for their Heart Attack Special—I mean, quarter-pounder with shake and fries.

J: If I were a cannibal, I'd probably think it is perfectly natural to eat *you*.

F: Oh, please! We're humans, they're animals.

J: Last I checked we were animals, too.

F: You know what I mean. We're special!

J: I'm sure that all animals are special to themselves. Anyway, all animals feel pain. No animal wants to die.

K: What if they don't see it coming? Besides, who's to say that cabbages or pineapples want to end up on your plate either? If you start worrying about that, you're going to starve to death.

G: You can argue all you want about cabbages or whatever, but what about cats and dogs? Would you eat your cat? People do, in some parts of the world.

K: That's sick.

H: You guys need to lighten up! Nobody's telling you what you have to eat. So for God's sake just live and let live—enjoy your food and quit arguing!

NOTES

For more on all of the points in this chapter, see my book *A 21st Century Ethical Toolbox* (second edition, New York: Oxford University Press; 2007), Chapter 1 ("Ethics as a Learning Experience," Chapter 2 ("Ethics-Avoidance Disorders"), and Chapter 4 ("Ethical Talk: Ground Rules").

For a first sense of the range of ethics and an introduction to some philosophical resources in ethics, check out Lawrence H. Hinman's "Ethics Updates" website at http://ethics.sandiego.edu/. For example, select the "Ethical Relativism" link for articles and general definitions. Hinman's site covers a wide range of issues and offers a guide to other Web-based ethics resources and a useful glossary of key terms in ethics.

On dogmatism, see Joshua Halberstam's book *Everyday Ethics: Inspired Solutions to Real-Life Dilemmas* (New York: Penguin; 1993), especially Chapter X—an interesting and opinionated complement to this one.

2

BEYOND AUTHORITY

Chapter 1 invites us to *think* about ethical issues. Moral questions are not to be pushed aside or avoided but welcomed and embraced, and there is much to learn in the process.

Fair enough. But it may seem—certainly we're often told—that most of our ethical thinking is already done for us: by moral rules or religious commandments. It is our job only to *apply* them. Questioning those rules or commandments, or expecting ambiguity and complexity, may be discouraged or even forbidden.

And yet, once again, for better or worse, things are not quite so simple. Philosophical ethics says: ethical thinking must be more open-ended. Neither rules nor commandments are enough by themselves. Ethics calls on each of us to think for ourselves.

THE LIMITS OF RULES

Rules—not just moral rules but all sorts of rules—are useful across the board. In fact, they are necessary. Life is too complicated to think through everything, every time, from the beginning. Rules are rough and ready provisional guides that allow us to get on, well enough, most of the time. "Better safe than sorry." "Better late than never." "If it's not broken, don't fix it."

But we understand very well that rules like these are only rough guides. They have exceptions. Sometimes late is worse than never. Safety may become such an obsession that we may end up safe *and* sorry. We understand that these rules are not meant to take the place of thinking— only to give thinking a place to start.

Moreover, such rules may conflict. If it is not broken, don't fix it—but then again, an ounce of prevention is worth a pound of cure. Maybe we're better safe than sorry—but then again, nothing ventured, nothing gained. In short, rules like these do not—and cannot—replace thinking. They are useful aids, nothing more. We still have to decide whether and how far they apply.

Conflicts and Exceptions

Despite their hoarier reputation, moral rules are arguably much the same. Take honesty. Certainly we have moral rules requiring us to tell the truth. Yet we also know that even such basic moral rules have exceptions. You *should* lie, for example, to save an innocent victim. We celebrate people who sheltered fugitives from the Nazis during the 1930s and 1940s in Europe, and people who sheltered fugitive slaves from slave-owners during the era of slavery in

America, even though these acts meant huge risks and systematic deception—nothing so slight as a single lie—sometimes for years.

Jean Valjean, hero of Victor Hugo's *Les Miserables*, was sentenced to hard labor for ten years because he stole a loaf of bread to feed his starving child. Certainly we have a rule that prohibits stealing—check out the Ten Commandments. But here too the rule is not the end of the story. For Valjean, it is only the beginning (also for Hugo: *Les Miserables* is a very long book!). We also have a rule that tells us to safeguard our children, and preserving their lives is certainly one of the most basic things ways we must do so. These two rules conflicted. Jean Valjean had to make a choice—and once again, despite the fact that this choice was actually against the law as well as against a commandment, we honor him for it.

In short, then, moral rules have exceptions and conflicts, just like everyday rules. For better or worse, they cannot do our thinking for us. Indeed, the person who insists on following such rules in every circumstance, without question, is the kind of person Mark Twain once called, "A good man in the worst sense of the term." Ethics asks more of us than that.

Ambiguity and Authority

There is another philosophical difficulty with an "automatic" view of moral rules as well. The *application* of moral rules is much more open-ended than it may seem at first.

Take the Golden Rule. It is certainly hard to quarrel with "Do unto others as you would have them do unto you" as a general guide to living. But in a way that is just the problem. The Golden Rule is a general guide to living, not a way to make specific decisions. To say "Do unto others as you would have them do unto you" is really to say: remember that, in the big picture, others are just as real, just as conscious, just as important as yourself. The rule only says that you should always bear that in mind. Good idea! But the rule does not say anything specific about what we should *do*. (Steal bread to feed my kids? Not, maybe, if I think about it as the baker. But as a starving kid...?) Once again, even with such rules—golden ones, too—we must decide how to apply them.

The existentialist philosopher Jean-Paul Sartre wrote about one of his students in occupied Paris during the Second World War who had to decide between staying with his dependent mother in Paris or escaping to England to fight in the war. Commenting on the decision, Sartre writes:

> Who could help him choose? [The rules that say we should] "be charitable, love your neighbor, take the more rugged path, etc."? But which is the more rugged path? Whom should he love as a [neighbor]? The fighting man or his mother? Which does the greater good, the vague act of fighting in a group, or the concrete one of helping a particular human being to go on living?

"[Rules] are vague," Sartre concludes, "and . . . always too broad for the specific and concrete case we are considering." Rules may give us a general orientation, but how to apply them remains up to us. Sometimes also, as in this case, more than one rule applies—that is, part of the choice itself is figuring out what rule to finally follow. In the end, once again, we have to choose.

There is a still more basic point as well. Sometimes we must ask about the authority of the rules themselves. Not all of our rules—even our moral rules—may really be good rules. Sometimes our moral rules need rethinking. After all, we inherit many of those rules from past societies, who we know were (let's just say) less than perfect in some ways. Their needs and perceptions may not match ours (not that we are perfect either, of course: we're just trying to keep learning...). Sometimes, yes, the old rules remind us of the really vital things. That the best things in life are free, for example, is easy to forget in our age of rampant consumerism. Other times, though, the old rules are genuinely questionable. For example, the fact that almost all of our traditional moral rules tend to slight other animals, and totally ignore the Earth as a whole, is now giving us pause.

So far from just "following the rules," then, we may sometimes have to rethink and even *change* the rules. And even if we reaffirm the old rules in the end, thinking them through is still our responsibility. We cannot pretend that we have no choice, that there is no question about the rules or which to choose or how to apply them. The reality is more demanding—and more interesting.

ETHICS AND THE LAW

Another appeal to authority that can arise in ethics is an appeal to the *law*. It is sometimes said that to act ethically we just need to follow the law. Is it so?

Following the law is usually moral as far as it goes. Some laws protect us and other people from harm, or buttress certain kinds of promises, like formal contracts and marriage vows. Here the law speaks to some of our basic needs and legitimate expectations—which, as you'll recall, brings it into the moral realm by definition.

The law also carries a certain moral weight just because it is the law. In a well-functioning democracy, at least, law is the outcome of democratic processes, and a certain basic respect for law is therefore a way of respecting each other—the moral community as a whole. Respect for the law may be necessary to maintain social order and therefore to protect many other things that we value. Political philosophers argue that because each of us benefits from others' respect for the law, we therefore owe it, and them, our respect as well.

None of this, though, shows that ethics can be reduced to following the law. For one thing, following the law is not *enough* for ethics. You could follow the law to the letter and still be a moral Scrooge. The law is actually rather minimal when it comes to moral matters. It insists on certain basics, often negative ones. It prohibits certain harms. But there it stops—as probably it should. The law prohibits theft but does not require us to give to charity. "Good Samaritan Laws" protect those who choose to try to help the injured or ill stranger, but they do not require us to help (except for doctors). Ethics often asks us to go us further.

So far from the law determining morality, in fact, it is more as if morality shapes the law (or, anyway, some of it—some parts of the law just do not concern moral matters at all). After all, the point of ethics is to consider what the law *should* say about assisted suicide or gay marriage or genetically modified organisms or the social obligations of business executives. We make laws *based*, in part, on ethics. Laws don't come out of the blue, after all—they come from our values!

Then again, a final difficulty for the moral authority of the law is that the law can also sometimes be morally wrong. Think of laws enforcing racial segregation or laws in many countries that prohibit people from gathering or communicating freely. At least the question must sometimes be asked: are these laws really good, right, fair? *Should* the law permit abortion in the early stages of pregnancy or allow the release of long-lived toxins into the environment or refuse sanction to gay marriage? If law simply determined morality, these questions could not even be asked. They would make no sense. But in fact they, and many others like them, can be and are asked, all the time. So far from the law simply determining moral values, the law may well need moral changes.

THE LIMITS OF COMMANDMENTS

Consider next the question of moral commandments, such as the Ten Commandments and other commands of God as reported in the Bible or asserted by some modern religious leaders. It may seem that here, at least, we have a kind of moral "rule" that applies without question or ambiguity. In fact, though, it turns out that many of the very same limits apply. With moral commandments, too, for many of the same reasons, thinking for ourselves is necessary. And even the Bible actually tells us so.

Ambiguity and Interpretation

We have noted that even the seemingly clearest moral rules can be ambiguous and unclear. Sartre points out that rules can be too vague to make decisions for us. The same is true, in just the same way, of commandments. "You shall not kill," for instance, seems about as clear as you can get. But many Christians and Jews support capital punishment—certainly a form of killing. Most fight in wars. Some also believe that suicide (self-killing) may sometimes be permissible, too. Most Christians and Jews eat other animals, which also requires killing on a massive scale. Apparently, there is a lot of ambiguity still.

Newer Protestant translations and most Jewish versions translate the commandment as "You shall not murder." This may seem more reasonable: it is at least arguable that killing in war or in the electric chair is not murder (although it is also arguable that it is) and the notion of murder is implicitly limited to humans (although it is arguable that it should not be). But the translation remains unsettled. The arguments on both sides are subtle. One way or the other we are back to, well, interpretation.

We are commanded to honor the Sabbath. But when is the Sabbath? Jews celebrate Shabbat from Friday sundown until Saturday sundown. Early Christians followed Jewish practice, only later shifting the observance to Sundays (mainly to distinguish themselves from Jews). Some Christians—Seventh-Day Adventists—still celebrate Sabbath on Saturdays, but midnight to midnight and not sundown to sundown. Is there a "right" answer? Not in the text!

Selective Obedience

There are also many explicit commandments that almost no one takes seriously and almost all of us feel free to ignore. Not too many people actually honor the Sabbath any more, come to think of it, whenever we take it to be. Here are a few more dramatic examples from *Leviticus*:

> 11:7: "You shall not eat the swine; it is unclean to you."
>
> 11:11-12: "Everything in the waters that has not fins and scales is an abomination to you. Of their flesh you shall not eat, and their carcasses you shall have in abomination."
>
> 19:9-10: "When you reap the harvest of your land, you shall not reap your field to its very border ... and you shall not strip your vineland bare, neither shall you gather the fallen

grapes of your vineyard; you shall leave them for the poor and the sojourner."

19:19: "There shall not come upon you a garment of cloth made of two kinds of stuff."

19:27: "You shall not round off the hair on your temples or mar the edges of your beard."

A few people—some Orthodox Jews, some Amish orders—actually do follow (some of) these commandments, but almost all other Christians and Jews disregard them entirely. Even confronted with explicit commandments, then, it seems that we still feel free to go our own way—if, for example, we think that some of these commands are just "historical relics," as many people say, like dietary restrictions that once made sense but are no longer necessary.

The point is not that we are hypocritical. The point, once again, is that we can and do decide for ourselves—understanding, for example, that whatever the text literally says, it comes from a historical place very unlike our own and is also the product of contentious translations and interpretations and therefore may apply differently to our time or may not apply at all. Even if we decide to follow its commands, that is still a *decision*—our decision.

This is not just an abstract point. Here is another passage from the same part of *Leviticus*:

20:13: "If a man lies with a man as with a woman, it is an abomination."

This commandment is regularly cited by people who claim that "God hates homosexuality." But these very same people, like almost all of the rest of us, disregard almost all of the rest of *Leviticus*. Where I live, certain churches even

hold pig roasts at rallies where speakers rail against homosexuality and other modern sins. If you read the text literally, though, God hates pig-eating just as much as He
hates (male) homosexuality. And if you do not read the
text literally, as seems reasonable enough in the case of
pig-eating, you cannot claim that you have no choice but
to take it literally in cases where it happens to accord with
your own preexisting moral convictions. In neither case,
really, is even an explicit commandment the end of the
story. *We* still decide about its ultimate application and
authority. And there are compelling arguments for different readings.

Questions of Authority

Religions in general aim to speak to us from the standpoint
of the sacred, the divine—from a place that stands beyond
the purely social and the momentary. This is a lofty and
precious thing. We need to hear that kind of voice.

On the other hand, for the very same reason, that kind
of voice is hard to hear clearly. We listen through profoundly limited filters. Thus, religions differ, sometimes
dramatically, depending on the time and place of their
origins and their particular histories and development
since then—and, of course, God is heard differently
within each of the major religions as well. One result is
that one religion's ethics may command one thing and
another religion's ethics may command another thing. At
the very least, this implies that appeals to one religion's
God cannot settle matters when people of other religions,
or no religion, are involved, as in our society at large. No

single religion (or any single interpretation within any specific religion) can claim automatic authority.

We will always struggle with partial perspective. Despite the heroism of some individual ministers, for instance, white churches were not notably out in front in the civil rights struggle. They were not notably behind, either, but that's just the point: they reflected their society. Historically, in fact, many churches supported slavery, even citing Biblical passages to defend slavery, such as these unfortunate lines from *Exodus* 21:

> When you buy a Hebrew slave, he shall serve six years, and in the seventh he shall go out free, for nothing. If he comes in single, he shall go out single; if he comes in married, his wife shall go out with him... . [But] when a man sells his daughter as a slave, she shall not go out as the male slaves do... . When a man strikes his slave, male or female, with a rod and the slave dies under his hand, he shall be punished. But if the slave survives a day or two, he is not to be punished; for the slave is his money.

Now, with slavery's evil recognized, the rationalization is transparent. Yet the words are there. Literally, the text does not say that slavery is wrong. It condones certain kinds of slavery under pretty broad conditions.

We may appreciate the writers of *Exodus* for trying to adapt a living ethical tradition to the needs of the time. Maybe these rules promised some improvement over slavery as it had been practiced earlier. But now, of course, times have changed. We still have a living tradition (in fact, *many* living traditions), but the needs of three thousand years ago are no longer our needs. We need to rethink and adapt the tradition just as the prophets and lawgivers of Biblical times did. And that may mean that we need to go beyond their words to the *spirit* of their acts and of our shared tradition—as clearly we have done long ago in the case of these words about slavery—even though ambiguity and uncertainty remain. Again, there is no refuge in the text. There is no alternative but to take the responsibility—of listening, interpreting, and, then, deciding—for ourselves.

LET THE STORIES BE STORIES

Many stories have a moral point. Enduring childhood stories like "The Boy Who Cried Wolf" make simple moral maxims memorable. Literary classics like *Les Miserables* illustrate moral complexities and ideals. Such stories are valuable learning tools, constant reminders, and guideposts when things get tough. Yet we also know that they are far from the moral last word. The same complications come up: we need to interpret and apply them, to decide for ourselves when they conflict, and to inquire into their final moral authority. This is part of what makes them so interesting.

The world's religious traditions are a prime source of moral stories as well. Those stories are often especially fascinating and deep. But again, precisely because stories like these are so rich, poetic, and complex, they seldom yield clear, specific guidance in specific situations. The same complications come up once again. Thus, what these stories really invite is (surprise!) more *thinking*.

Consider, for example, the Bible's story of the destruction of Sodom.

> The two angels came to Sodom in the evening; and Lot was sitting in the gate of Sodom. When Lot saw them, he rose to meet them ... and said, "My lords, turn aside, I pray you, to your servant's house, and spend the night, and wash your

feet; then you may rise up early and go on your way." ... He urged them strongly; so they turned aside to him and entered his house; and he made them a feast, and baked unleavened bread, and they ate.

But before they lay down, the men of the city, the men of Sodom, both young and old, all the people to the last man, surrounded the house, and they called to Lot, "Where are the men who came to you tonight? Bring them out to us, that we may know [i.e. rape] them." Lot went out of the door to the men, shut the door after him, and said, "I beg you, my brothers, do not act so wickedly... . Do nothing to these men, for they have come under the shelter of my roof. Behold, I have two daughters who have not known man; let me bring them out to you, and do to them as you please; only do nothing to these men, for they have come under the shelter of my roof." But [the crowd] said, "Stand back!" ... Then they pressed hard against Lot, and drew near to break the door. But [the angels] put forth their hands and drew Lot into the house to them, and shut the door. And they struck with blindness the men who were at the door of the house, so that they wearied themselves groping for the door (*Genesis* 19:1–11).

God destroys the city the next day, after helping Lot and his family to flee.

You probably know that this is a widely cited and contentious story. Yet it is also quite a puzzling and disturbing story once you read it carefully.

What actually *is* the true sin of Sodom? One traditional reading insists that it is homosexuality. And it is true that homosexual acts (of a sort) are in the story. Other verses can be cited in support of this reading as well, such as the verse from *Leviticus* cited earlier and the letters of Paul in the New Testament.

Nonetheless, the insistence that *the* sin *must* be homo-sexuality—that no other reading is even possible, and no other possible sin matters—misses the depth of the story itself. An ancient reading is that the true crimes of Sodom are its shocking level of violence and its extreme disrespect for strangers. That's certainly in the story, too—in fact, one might have thought it is a lot more central to it.

The prophet Ezekiel had another interpretation: "Behold, this was the guilt of ... Sodom: she and her daughters had pride, surfeit of food, and prosperous ease, but did not aid the poor and needy" (*Ezekiel* 16:49). On this view, the story is really a call to social justice!

You and I might suppose that if anything is specifically condemned in this story, it is rape. After all, rape is what the Sodomites had on their minds. But we cannot stop there either. Lot, who is presented as the only decent man in Sodom, actually offers the crowd his own daughters in the place of his guests. "Do to them as you please," he says. The angels prevent these rapes, too, from happening. But God still saves Lot from the destruction of the rest of the city. Does not Lot's willingness to offer his own daughters to be brutalized offend God? Why is *this* not "wicked"—in the extreme?

We are reminded that this story was written at a time when some values were very different than they are now: when, for one thing, women were regarded only as a father's or husband's property, for him to dispose of as he saw fit. However we interpret the story, then, it becomes harder to take it as any kind of moral last word.

In any case, again, the main point can hardly be said to be *clear.* You begin to see why, for some religious traditions, exploring the interpretation of such stories is the core of worship itself. Christians inherit long traditions of debate and disagreement about Scripture, and Judaism's second most sacred text, the Talmud, is essentially a record of loving disputation about the Torah and its stories. Learning to see the depth and complexity in these stories is a form of moral learning, too: we can come to see the same sort of depth and complexity in the moral situations that confront us in our actual lives.

THINKING FOR YOURSELF

God came to Elijah when he was hiding out in despair, alone, in a cave at Mount Horeb. And there, the Bible says, God spoke in a "still, small voice" (I *Kings* 19:12)—a phrase that can also be translated as "gentle breeze," "soft whisper," "hardly a sound." A hiss, a rustle.

What a remarkable image! It seems that the Bible itself is telling us here that hearing that voice can be a very tricky thing—and in any case it comes to each of us, very quietly, almost imperceptibly, on our own. You begin to see why Quakers and many others, both religious and secular, put their livelihoods and even their lives on the line for freedom of conscience. Protestant Christianity began with the insistence that everyone should be able to read and interpret the Scriptures for themselves. God speaks quietly, to each of us, and often in our individual moments of reflection and concentration. Surely, then, religious ethics ought to *honor* thinking for oneself.

Some people may find it hard to reconcile such a message with the experience of tight-knit religious communities in which the leaders fervently believe that they speak for God Himself and therefore *do* expect obedience. They may even explicitly forbid critical thinking, and even when it is tolerated it is seldom appreciated or allowed to go very far. Not only is it hard to buck such insistent and accepted authority—it can also be hard to question leaders who you respect and may even love.

Still, though—one last time—there is a deep wisdom in what ethics asks. We can see this best by looking to the wisest of the wise.

Think of the Hindu Mahatma Gandhi, the Sufi (Islamic mystic) poet Rumi, or the philosopher Socrates. Think of

South Africa's Nelson Mandela, a resolutely secular man who nonetheless deeply respects religion, and Archbishop Desmond Tutu, whose life is committed within the Anglican Church, who together did what everyone thought impossible: peacefully bring democracy to their country.

These are great people. And they do not avoid moral issues—often they wade right in. They may advise us. They may attempt to persuade us, as may any respected and loved moral leader.

But here is the crucial thing: none of these people would claim to speak for God, or demand that you put their judgment in place of your own. On the contrary, they are acutely and humbly aware of their own limits as well as the limits of others. They recognize that, even with the best of intentions, they are still creatures of their time and place, and therefore that *even they* will hear the voice of God through the filters of partial understanding or the residues of local prejudice or the lack of the full range of human experience. So they lead by inspiring *more* thinking—not less. They ask for respect of a different and more critical kind. And that, actually, is how they make a moral difference—not by dictating, in the name of God or anything else, what we ought to do.

"Shall not the Judge of all the Earth do right?"

Remember another part of the Sodom story—a part seldom cited by would-be moral authorities, but a part nonetheless, and in fact right next to the episode just quoted. On the angels' way to Sodom, they visit the patriarch Abraham in his desert tent. As they leave, they declare God's intention to destroy Sodom if the rumors about it are true. But Abraham is troubled by this. He cannot see the justice of killing the innocent along with the wicked. So Abraham, says the Bible, "went before the Lord."

> Abraham drew near and said: "Wilt thou indeed destroy the righteous with the wicked? Suppose there are fifty righteous within the city; wilt thou then destroy the place and not spare it for the fifty righteous who are in it? Far be it from thee to do such a thing, to slay the righteous with the wicked, so that the righteous fare as the wicked! Far be that from thee! Shall not the Judge of all the Earth do right?"
>
> And the Lord said, "If I find at Sodom fifty righteous in the city, I will spare the whole place for their sake." Abraham answered, "Behold, I have taken upon myself to speak to the Lord, I who am but dust and ashes. Suppose five of the fifty righteous are lacking. Wilt thou destroy the whole city for lack of five?" And He said, "I will not destroy it if I find forty-five there." Again he spoke to him, and said, "Suppose forty are found there." He answered, "For the sake of forty I will not do it." Then he said, "Oh let not the Lord be angry, and I will speak. Suppose thirty are found there." He answered, "I will not do it, if I find thirty there." He said, "Behold, I have taken upon myself to speak to the Lord. Suppose twenty are found there." He answered, "For the sake of twenty I will not destroy it."
>
> Then [Abraham] said, "Oh let not the Lord be angry, and I will speak again but this once. Suppose ten are found there." The Lord answered, "For the sake of ten I will not destroy it." And the Lord went his way, when he had finished speaking to Abraham; and Abraham returned to his place.

What is the Bible telling us here? Surely not that we should simply do what we're told, and accept whatever authority—even the absolutely highest authority of all—decides to do. Quite the contrary. Abraham, the revered forefather, would not accept what seemed to him to be injustice even when God Himself proposed to do it. Abraham went to God—Abraham who knew himself to be "but dust and ashes" in the eyes of God—and questioned and challenged. "Shall not the Judge of all the Earth do right?"

So Abraham thought for himself—and spoke up, too. Moreover, God listened and answered. Indeed Lot was saved, the Bible says later, because God was "mindful of Abraham." Now there is a story to live up to! The next time you're told not to think for yourself but just to obey, then, or to do what someone else tells you is the right thing or the will of God (according to them)—*remember Abraham.*

FOR PRACTICE

Review

Begin by summarizing and reviewing the main points of this chapter. What are the limits to the authority of moral rules? To the moral authority of the law? Why is thinking for oneself necessary even when we are given explicit commands of God as reported in the Bible? What may we learn from Abraham's example?

More Moral Stories

It may take some practice to approach the familiar moral stories with an eye for complexity and nuance rather than for a single moral lesson they are supposed to teach. Yet the skill of interpreting stories in this open-ended way is nothing new. In your education, you may have encountered it in the interpretation of literature. Originally, it was developed by ancient and medieval Biblical scholars, both Christian and Jewish, for the interpretation of Scripture (where it is often called "hermeneutics"). Interpretations—of the

Bible or *Les Miserables* or anything else—may be better or worse, more or less inclusive or systematic or fertile, but whatever else they may be, they are very seldom simple!

In fact, it seems to be a striking feature of spiritual teachings in general that they so often take the form of stories, especially stories that seem to open up complexities rather than simplify things. Jesus constantly spoke in parables (and his disciples constantly complain about it—don't you think it is interesting that the Bible reports this?). So do the Sufi masters (Islamic mystics), the Hasids (Jewish mystics), and the Zen masters (Buddhists). Why do you think this might be? If there really is one right answer, why don't they just tell us?

It may be easier to develop your interpretive skills with stories that are less familiar. Try some. For Sufi stories, go to Idries Shah's collection, *Tales of the Dervishes* (New York: Penguin, 1970). For African moral parables, try Moharnrned Naseehu Ali's *The Prophet of Zongo Street* (New York: Amistad Press, 2006). The philosopher Martin Buber collected volumes of Hasidic tales in *Tales of the Hasidim* (New York: Schocken, 1991). And classic Zen stories can be found in *Zen Flesh, Zen Bones,* compiled by Paul Reps and Nyogen Senzaki (Boston: Shambhala, 1994).

To begin your practice, here is an 800-year-old parable from the Sufi (Islamic mystic) master Yusuf of Andalusia.

Nuri Bey was a respected and reflective Albanian, who married a wife much younger than himself. One evening when he had returned home earlier than usual, a faithful servant came to him and said: "Your wife is acting suspiciously. She is in her apartments with a huge chest, large enough to hold a man ... . It should contain only a few ancient embroideries. I believe that there may now be much more in it ... ."

Nuri went to his wife's room, and found her sitting disconsolately beside the massive wooden box. "Will you show me what is in the chest?" he asked.

"Because of the suspicion of a servant, or because you do not trust me?"

"Would it not be easier just to open it, without thinking about the undertones?" asked Nuri.

"I do not think it possible."

"Where is the key?"

She held it up. "Dismiss the servant and I will give it to you."

The servant was dismissed. The woman handed over the key and herself withdrew, obviously troubled in mind. Nuri Bey thought for a long time. Then he called four gardeners from his estate. Together they carried the chest by night unopened to a distant part of the grounds, and buried it. The matter was never referred to again.

Of course we want to know what was in the chest. But it seems to be the whole point of the story that we, like Nuri Bey, are not to know. We are left with other questions. Is his act a wise one? Does the story mean to suggest that it is? He doesn't push the point—he doesn't open the chest—but he apparently doesn't entirely trust his wife either. Or in burying the chest is his idea to also bury mistrust—is he still trying to avoid the "undertones"? Would his wife agree that he succeeded at this?

And—after all—what was in the box? Is it obvious that his wife is hiding a lover? Could it be something else—a present, maybe, that he is not quite ready for yet? Some other kind of magical possibility that his jealousy and fear "bury" for him? Notice that for her the issue is trust. She withdraws "troubled in mind" but not in denial or defiance. What do you make of that? Is he the real moral hero—or is she?

God and the Good

Since Abraham asks "Shall not the Judge of all the Earth do right?" he clearly does not think that values are literally defined by God's commands. If God's commands simply define the good, then "the Judge of all the Earth" does right by definition, and the question would be senseless. Many people find such a view troubling because it makes values seem arbitrary.

Instead, it seems that Abraham questions God on the basis of independent moral standards. Even God must "do right"—not whatever He pleases. But this may seem troubling for other reasons. For one thing, how did Abraham know that it is wrong to kill the innocent, even if God Himself were to do it? Think about that question for a while. If you are reading this book in an ethics class, some of your other readings may suggest some answers.

For another thing, if God does not define the good, then mustn't the good in some sense define God? It may not surprise you that theologians and philosophers have been thinking about that question for several thousand years. Most, although not all, answer Yes—in some sense. As to how this might be possible, ask your local theologian.

NOTES

The quote from Jean-Paul Sartre is from "Existentialism," in *Existentialism and Human Emotions* (New York: Philosophical Library, 1957, p. 25). Bible quotations are from the Revised Standard Version (New York: National Council of Churches of Christ in America, 1952). "The Ancient Coffer of Nuri Bey" comes from Idries Shah, *Tales of the Dervishes* (New York: Penguin, 1970).

In Plato's *Euthyphro,* the Greek philosopher Socrates carefully analyzes the relation of the good to the gods and argues, as this book does, that an independent judgment of values is inescapable. For a rigorous contemporary discussion of the problem, see James Rachels, *The Elements of Moral Philosophy* (New York: McGraw-Hill Companies, many editions, Chapter 4).

On current issues in religion and ethics, see the website of the PBS series "Religion and Ethics Newsweekly" (http://www.pbs.

org/wnet/religionandethics/). Peggy Morgan and Clive Lawton's *Ethical Issues in Six Religious Traditions* (Edinburgh: Edinburgh University Press, 2006) offers a thorough and even-handed overview of each tradition's basic approach. A complementary brief for non-religious morality is Walter Sinnott-Armstrong's *Morality without God* (New York: Oxford University Press, 2009). For further philosophical issues between ethics and religion, the Ethics Updates website offers extensive resources at http://ethics.sandiego.edu/theories/Religion/index.asp.

3

ETHICAL THEORIES

∽

Chapter 1 defined moral values as those values that give voice to the basic needs and legitimate expectations of others as well as ourselves. Moral values connect us to a larger world ("the needs of others as well as ourselves") and introduce the question of what others are entitled to ask from us, as well as what we are entitled to ask from them ("legitimate expectations").

But we hold a *lot* of moral values so understood. Fairness, equality, respect, and responsibility; reducing pain and suffering; "life, liberty, and the pursuit of happiness"; humility, benevolence, keeping your promises; honesty, responsibility, community, dignity ... and that is only a barest beginning of a list. We might well feel overwhelmed. How can we discern any kind of forest—a bigger and hopefully clearer picture, more order and less confusion—amidst all these trees?

SYSTEMATIZING MORAL VALUES

Philosophy's answer is an attempt to work out *systems* of moral values. The aim is to find some unifying threads to our apparently diverse moral values. For example, many of our moral values are related to fairness, equality, and justice. Perhaps we could find some elegant and clear way of drawing them together, some relatively simple criterion or bottom line? If these values do in fact form a sort of "family," then surely there should be some sort of "family resemblance," so to speak. Wouldn't it be helpful to know what it is?

Or again, many moral values have to do with personal virtues, like honesty, humility, and self-possession. Again, perhaps there is some relatively clear and focused human ideal that connects these different virtues, giving each a logical place in a single, unified picture. We would understand all the virtues better if we could paint that bigger picture with confidence and clarity.

You begin to see the hope: that we might discover that many of our moral values actually *hang together* in basic ways. There may be deep connections between moral values that can bring some order to the confusion that may strike us at first. In the simplest way, then, the aim of what philosophers call *ethical theories* is to seek and bring out these sorts of patterns and connections: that is, to (try to!) systematize moral values.

Working from Within

Such theories speak to our practice: they aim to improve, to clarify, and to guide it. But they do so in a very different and (usually) much more modest way than the rules and commandments considered in the last chapter. Rules and commandments claim to speak from an external and authoritative standpoint, and they aim to simplify our moral choices, if not values, by just telling us what to do. Ethical theories, by contrast, work from *within* the many and diverse values we ourselves already hold, and aim to help us find our way by working out deeper connections and patterns within those very values themselves.

The term "theory" is a good clue here. Theories by definition do not assert some final and complete knowledge that others must simply accept and obey. The project of theory is, instead, ongoing and exploratory, open to debate and alternative views—as in the social sciences, for example, which also attempt to find deeper patterns, underlying connections, in everyday, familiar things, especially when those patterns are not evident at first or on the surface.

Ethical theory's aim, then, is not to somehow replace the need to think for ourselves. On the contrary: ethical theory is a *way* of thinking for ourselves—a ongoing process of trying to discern the broader patterns that hold within our values, to be judged by how much sense they in fact manage to make of our values, carefully considered. Theory's main aim, in the end, is not to offer another set of dictates but instead greater *clarity*.

THREE ETHICAL THEORIES

Three ethical theories, speaking in turn for three general families of moral values, are the most central in philosophical ethics today. Each brings with it an involved and continuing debate, as you might imagine, but each main idea can still be sketched with a few quick strokes.

The Ethics of Happiness

Perhaps our most familiar and natural family of moral values focuses on *happiness*. We all seek pleasure, and not just in a crude or narrow sense: true happiness is not just, or even mainly, a matter of gratified senses, but it is more settled and longer-term, a matter of fulfilled purpose and self-possession. We also understand that a happy life is not a matter of happiness or pleasure at every moment. There are tradeoffs: certain periods of displeasure or even pain (hard exercise, maybe) for greater happiness over the long run (health). Our greatest *net* happiness—the great balance of happiness over pain or suffering in the long run—is the rational aim.

With one more step, however, this relaxed and commonsensical practical framework can become a systematic ethical theory. The key additional claim is this: happiness is essentially *social*. We naturally seek the well-being of others as well as ourselves: our spouses, children, and parents as well as our friends, co-workers, fellow citizens, and on and on. We're sometimes tempted to think that "everyone is selfish," but actually we know very well that true egoists live crabbed, cramped, and unhappy lives—and also that they are few and far between. Our own happiness is bound up with the happiness of others.

Besides, to say that happiness is a good thing is not just to make a claim about one's own happiness. Ethics by definition, remember, points us to the well-being of others as well as of ourselves. From a moral point of view I cannot say that your happiness is of no concern to me simply because I'm me, so to speak, and you're you. No: happiness *as such* is a morally good thing, wherever it occurs—and it is good in the same way and to the same extent.

Ethics, therefore, moves us from a preoccupation with our own well-being or happiness to a concern with the well-being or happiness of others as well. Make of this a more quantitative, calculating conception, and we arrive at the ethical theory called *utilitarianism*. Two nineteenth-century English thinkers, Jeremy Bentham and John Stuart Mill, are credited as its founders. Bentham's famous standard is "the greatest good of the greatest number." Now it is the greatest net *social* happiness—the great balance of happiness over pain or suffering in society as a whole, in the long run—that is the rational aim.

Bentham actually imagined that we could one day solve moral problems by sitting down with a calculator and figuring up the amounts of pleasure, for everyone involved, on either side. Modern economic thinking sometimes has a similar hope. We wish to use our often-limited resources to benefit as many people as we can with the lowest costs to others—seeking the greatest net benefit to, broadly speaking, social welfare—and sometimes, at least, relative benefits are calculable.

The Ethics of the Person

An equally important thread running through our moral values is an insistence on honoring *persons:* that unique, self-conscious, and self-determining kind of being who holds a unique and compelling moral value as a result.

In his book *I and Thou*, the twentieth-century German/Israeli philosopher Martin Buber famously described the encounter with persons so understood. Too often, says Buber, we "go over the surface of the world" and just "pile up information" without really going to the depths of anything. Other people seem to be just objects—a person viewed this way is an "It," as Buber puts it—pleasant or annoying or useful but still no different than cars or rocks or boxes of chocolate. But there is also another way to relate to others. To encounter another person as a "Thou" (or a "You") pulls us up short. Buber writes of this kind of encounter as if it strikes us with a "flash," like lightning. The "Thou," the Other, suddenly is transformed, is unpredictable, spontaneous, deep, infinite—way beyond just annoying or useful or whatever. Our own selves, our "I"—the other half of the "I/Thou" relationship—are then transformed, too. We can no longer stand apart but are wholly engaged with the other person, "submerged in their depths."

Buber admits that it is often necessary, day to day, to relate to other people partly as "Its." Still, it is the task of ethics to bring us back to a fundamental regard for persons as such, as supremely valuable "Thous." The moral and legal structures of rights, for example, are one way. Basic rights to life and liberty, along with social and political rights such as the right to free association, religion, and thought, are all ways of recognizing others as independent centers of thought and action, radically different than mere things. Equality also follows—for we are all equally persons, equally centers of worlds, beyond external differences of race or sex or class—thus grounding the moral and political quest for fairness and justice. Many systems of religious ethics also make the values of persons central, conceiving the human person as a model of God Himself ("made in His image")—an emphatic way of affirming our infinite preciousness and making it central to ethics.

The eighteenth-century German philosopher Immanuel Kant put it this way: persons are not just "means" but "ends in themselves." Kant puts his famous "categorical imperative"—the fundamental ethical principle, in his view—in exactly these terms:

> Always act so as to treat humanity, whether in yourself or in another, as an end and never merely as a means.

Unfortunately, we are treated like "means" all too often. Think of the cheery salesperson who greets you like a long-lost brother but then hangs up in midsentence as soon as it's clear he's not going to make a sale. More chilling cases are when a person feels reduced to mere means to someone else's sexual pleasure. "You're treating me like an object," we say. An ethic of the person helps us understand what has gone so profoundly wrong in cases like these— and points us in the right direction.

The Ethics of Virtue

A third family of moral values brings forward the *virtues*. The Greeks had their four great virtues—Prudence, Justice, Temperance, Courage. The medievals added Faith, Hope, and Charity to create the seven Cardinal Virtues known to every Catholic schoolchild. The even more famous Seven Deadly Sins are their opposites. We treasure Loyalty, Dependability, Humility. The Work Ethic, at its best, asks of us Persistence, Reliability, Thrift, Economy. In families, as the Chinese sage Confucius reminds us, the necessary virtues are Respect and Faithfulness.

But this is still only a list. Ethical philosophers, remember, will ask for more. We need a *theory* of the virtues: some overall, general explanation of why any of these character traits really are morally valuable. What *makes* a trait a virtue? What is Virtue in itself?

Aristotle—a fourth-century BCE Greek philosopher—proposed one classic answer. The key lies, he argued, in human nature itself. Everything in the world, according to Aristotle, has a distinctive and essential *function*. Plants and animals grow in special ways depending on their kinds. Craftspeople have their particular crafts. And in Aristotle's view, this function or activity in turn determines admirable or "excellent" characteristics or traits—that is, virtues. Virtue in a craftsperson, for example, is to practice the craft well: it takes deftness, attention, care, and productivity.

Similarly, then, there must be a characteristic or set of characteristics that defines *our* essence—the human "function" as such.

> For just as for a flute player, a sculptor, or any artist, and, in general, for all things that have a function or activity, the good and the "well" is thought to reside in the function, so it would seem to be for man ... .

In Aristotle's theory, then, the moral virtues are those character traits that fulfill our essence as human beings. They are, fully realized, the distinctive excellences of human beings. Since we are, in Aristotle's famous definition, *rational animals*, the virtues for humans must be those traits that express and help us to fulfill our rational nature, broadly understood: knowledge and understanding, in the life of the mind, along with the judiciousness and self-discipline to keep our more passionate side in balance. This balancing, on Aristotle's view, often requires finding the "mean" between the extremes of our passions.

We should try to act courageously, for example, which is the "Golden Mean" between the opposed excesses of rashness and cowardice.

Growing in all of these virtues together allows us to achieve our potential, to become fully human. Rightly understood, virtue is nothing less than the royal road to *becoming ourselves*.

ETHICAL THEORIES AT WORK

Ethical theories can help us deepen our understanding and clarify ethical issues in a variety of useful ways.

Grounding Ethical Arguments

One of the primary uses of ethical theories is to give us a way to ground specific ethical arguments in larger ethical frameworks and contexts. Families and communities and governments, for example, often make great efforts to reduce pain and suffering of all kinds and to build health, harmony, and peace. Utilitarianism expresses all of this as *ethical*. It is not just a matter of custom or good budgeting but part of our moral obligation to each other: to serve the collective good.

The ethics of the person, meanwhile, helps us understand moral precepts like the Golden Rule. It is because other people are equally *persons* that ethics requires taking a less self-centered point of view than we often do. Imagining how we would feel or what we would decide if the situation were reversed—if we were the "done to" rather than the doer—gives us a quick moral check on whether our act is appropriately respectful all the way around.

Kant takes this line of thought still further. In another and maybe even more famous form, his "Categorical Imperative" requires us to

Act only according to that maxim whereby you can at the same time will that it become a universal law.

By "maxim," Kant means, roughly, the rule you propose to yourself when trying to decide what to do. "Law" he means not in the legal sense but in the *universal* sense: a rule everyone could follow. Thus, Kant says, if I cannot will my maxim to be a rule that everyone follows, I am really just making an exception for myself. For example, if I lie to get out of a sticky situation, I rely on other people's practice of *not* lying even in such a tight spot— since if everyone else also lied in such situations, no one would believe me in mine. In this way, according to Kant, I am actually making "means" of other persons, treating myself as somehow different or special, rather than affirming myself as one among equals, everyone an end in themselves.

Aristotle's theory of virtue, for its part, gives a compelling grounding for many professional codes of ethics. Medical codes like the Hippocratic Oath enjoin doctors to serve life, to respect the privacy and vulnerability of sick people and their families, and above all to "do no harm." This might seem like just an accidental collection of moral norms. In fact, though, it is rooted directly in the nature of medical practice itself and its final aim— the health of the patient. The Hippocratic Oath derives from the *function* of medicine, just as Aristotle suggests. We can say much the same for journalists or teachers or auto mechanics. Many professions' codes of ethics point deeper to the "internal good" or ideal function of the profession itself.

Focusing Key Questions

Ethical theories can also sometimes focus the key questions in specific moral debates, especially when a moral debate falls primarily within one specific family of values and thus under the purview of one kind of theory. We think about the ethics of abortion, for example, primarily in terms of the ethics of persons. Here, not surprisingly, it turns out that the exact nature of a "person" itself is a key question. The personhood of pregnant women is a given, and many kinds of choices are certainly their rights. But is the fetus also a person? If so, it may have rights as well. We might therefore hope for some progress from a close and careful analysis of just what makes something a person.

This is no easy question, of course. Self-awareness is crucial to personhood in Kant's view, for example, which seems to exclude fetuses. Then again, we do consider comatose people still to be persons with rights, so it might be argued that Kant's definition is too narrow. What would be a better definition?

Another question is why we should assume that personhood must happen all at once. Couldn't it emerge slowly—suggesting, perhaps, a gradualistic approach to abortion rather than drawing a single all-or-nothing line? All of these are good questions, and although they are certainly difficult, they address a much more focused and (we might hope) more readily answerable question than the usual abortion debate as a whole.

Mapping Ethical Debates

Yet another use of ethical theories is, paradoxically, somewhat the opposite: to systematically remind us that multiple types of values are usually at stake in moral debates. We can understand some ethical issues precisely as conflicts between different ethical theories.

Regularly, for example, the ethics of the person—the ethics of rights or justice, especially—seems to be pitted against utilitarianism. Questions of censorship pit the right to free speech against the benefits of greater social cohesion or safety. Public restrictions on smoking or even fatty foods or going without health insurance, as are now being enacted in some places, limit liberty—so it's argued—in the name of public health.

North Carolina, my state, recently enacted a lottery. There is a clear social benefit—better education, since most of the money is supposed to go to the schools—so you could argue that the lottery should have the support of utilitarians. On the other hand, lotteries are forms of gambling, and therefore play to our vices, after all—the opposite of virtues—such as greed, impulsiveness, and irresponsibility. So while utilitarianism may say Yes, the ethics of virtue emphatically says No.

Where one of the theories is not yet represented in a debate, we could seek to bring it in. For example, what would the ethics of the person say about lotteries? Rights are relevant: our presumption usually is that we have a right to do anything that is not harmful to others. But justice turns out to be relevant, too. Since poorer people are the main target of lottery ticket sales, it is sometimes argued that the lottery really just amounts to another tax on the people who can least afford it. Aren't they therefore being used as means to other people's ends? And you could argue that it is a tax not just on their money but, as it were, on their hopes. Shouldn't the state be offering people *real* hopes rather than false ones?

Sorting out moral debates in this way does not necessarily make resolving them any easier. It may well make them harder! Part of the point of ethics is that moral issues *are* in fact complex—more involved and many-sided than we often think in the midst of debate about them, when things can get too simplified. More is at stake, and often enough there are genuine moral values on both (all) sides. Ultimately we can only resolve them if we begin by recognizing their complexity and depth.

Prompting Change

Finally, the logic of ethical theories can be relentless in pushing us toward new values and challenging and changing old habits and ideas. Theories can prompt moral rethinking and growth.

One of the challenges in defining *person* in general, for example, is that persons are not necessarily just human. Many other animals are much more developed and self-aware than human fetuses, certainly than fetuses in the early months of pregnancy. If we define personhood partly by degree of development or self-awareness, then, we may end up having to extend certain rights to other animals along with human fetuses or even to some other animals but *not* to fetuses. This may (or may not) strike you as a strange possibility, but the question, all the same, is a logical consequence of the path that the ethics of the persons starts you along. Now we are invited—even required—to figure out where that path leads.

Lately many utilitarians have also been paying attention to other animals. Here, too, the theory's logic seems to require it. Animals have pleasures and pains, too, and unfortunately some of their most extreme pains are inflicted by us. But if happiness is good wherever it occurs, and suffering is bad wherever it occurs, don't we need to consider the well-being of animals, too? Especially when their pain so dramatically exceeds our gains, it may be time to make some changes.

You see, then, that ethical theories do not leave you alone! Once again, there is no substitute for some good hard thinking.

SHOULDN'T ONE THEORY RULE?

Some philosophers argue that since the project of ethical theory is to unify values, we should aim to fit all moral values together into *one* single system in the end. Utilitarians, most notably, often argue that all ethics reduces (or should be reduced) to the Greatest Happiness Principle. Even rights and virtues, they suggest, are only good so far as they serve happiness—which they generally do, at least in the long run. But when we say that certain virtues are not *always* good, as we said about honesty in the last chapter, for example, aren't we really saying that there is a higher ultimate standard to which they must be held? And what could that standard be but the good of the whole?

Non-utilitarian philosophers respond that sometimes we choose other values over happiness. Not *any* lie is justified just because it makes people a little (or even a lot) happier. And the social good is not the last word when we are weighing up rights, like our free speech rights or the rights of accused criminals to fair trials even if cumbersome and costly.

It seems that each of the theories sometimes limits the others. The very fact that these theories have been contending for so long may also be a sign that they are tentative and partial. None rules every time. We can put the same point more positively, too. Ethical theories work best when they address *families* of moral values—subsets of moral values, not necessarily moral values as whole.

It is still possible that someday, maybe, a single ethical theory will successfully weave all moral values into a single theory. Some philosophers—maybe you too—will, and should, keep on trying. Still, there are dangers in investing too much in this hope. We can oversimplify values, for one thing, in our drive to make them fit. Or we may too readily dismiss values that do not fit our favored theory. And the demand for a single theory also can dramatically raise the stakes for our existing moral debates. Simple issues may start to look like battlefields between huge matters of principle, and then any kind of compromise or balanced resolution becomes much harder to achieve. Better, for practical purposes, to take ethical theories as limited tools. One theory should *not* rule!

But What about Decision making?

You know by now that it is not the aim of philosophical ethics to produce any kind of simple formula by which we can live without any further thinking. Quite the opposite: the point is precisely to *think*, and to keep thinking. Ethical theories, as I've tried to suggest, do their part in a variety of ways—and the multiplicity of ethical theories is crucial. From this point of view, the fact that a diversity of theories may sometimes make moral decision-making harder is not necessarily an objection. In a way, that is ethical theories' *job*. There *is* usually more to consider, and there is no automatic way to put it all together. Any good account of moral choices should reflect that fact.

Some people may worry that we therefore will be unable to make any intelligent decisions at all. But of course we can! We will see in the next chapter that there are perfectly fine and even familiar ways of making ethical decisions without any single theory or rule incorporating the other or necessarily taking precedence. A single theory is not necessary. Quite the contrary, once again: a more diverse and open-ended view of moral values arguably makes more constructive and creative moral decisions possible.

Some people also may fear that unless one theory rules, a certain kind of personal steadfastness or moral reliability will be hard to sustain. It's a matter of integrity, they say. If we don't follow a single lode-star, we might not always go in the same direction.

But integrity must not require oversimplifying values either. Remember that the core meaning of "integrity" is actually "wholeness." The imperative is to stay *whole*: inclusive, complete, wide-angled. Acknowledge that a variety of incompatible values are at stake, then, and keep them all in play consistently and constructively. As we will see in the next chapter, you can commit to the best of them and still chart a consistent and balanced course.

ETHICAL THEORIES AT A GLANCE

- The Ethics of *Happiness*, or *Utilitarianism*: Seek the "greatest good (happiness, fulfillment, well-being) of the greatest number."
- The Ethics of the *Person*: Honor unique, self-conscious, self-determining individuals, "ends in themselves" and not just "means."
- The Ethics of *Virtue*: Nurture the human excellences—those character traits that represent what is most fully human in us, such as justice, loyalty, and self-possession.

FOR PRACTICE

Review

Summarize and review the main points of this chapter. What is an ethical theory? Why is it not just another appeal to some kind of authority, like rules or commandments? Explain the three types of ethical theories outlined in this chapter. Illustrate their applications and other uses. How is it that they limit and complement each other?

You might also ask which of the three kinds of ethical theories outlined in this chapter speaks to you most directly. How might you put that theory in your own words? Why do you find it especially compelling? And why do the others speak to you less often or persuasively? How can you take better account of those other sorts of values, too?

Your classmates or friends will probably have different answers than yours. What do you think accounts for your differences?

Using the Theories

We have seen that ethical theories can help clarify contemporary moral debates. Here are some further controversies to consider in the same way. What does each theory say about them? Are the different theories' perspectives, and their contrasts, helpful? How?

- Should doctors always tell their patients the truth—even when, in the doctor's opinion, the truth may be too depressing for the patient to bear or may even prevent the patient from getting better?

- Many businesses and some nonprofit organizations now have codes of ethics. What types of moral values do such codes typically include? (You'll need to do some research.) What types of moral values do you think such a code should include? Might it be that a business code of ethics should only concern certain kinds of moral values and not others? Must business serve the social good, for example, or should businesspeople be judged only by their personal virtuousness?

- How would you go about constructing a student code of ethics? Review your own school's honor code, if you have one. Why does it say what it says? Is an honor code enough? What other kinds of ethical obligations do you think specifically apply to students? Why? Rewrite and expand your school's code and propose it to your student government and administrators. How will you argue for it?

- Try designing a company—or, if you're really ambitious, a whole economic or political system—without knowing what your own status will be within it. If you don't know whether you'll be a janitor or a CEO, a worker or an ordinary citizen, or a movie star or a homeless person, how will you set up your company's decision-making processes or your society's way of taking care of the needy? What ethical theories come into play here? Do they conflict?

- Should marijuana be legalized? What might each theory say? Why? Are there key factual questions in this debate that the theories help bring into focus? What questions?

- The utilitarian Jeremy Bentham was active as a prison and criminal law reformer. From a utilitarian point of view, the point of punishment is not to somehow exact revenge or retribution, but to serve the social good. This seems to argue for a more restorative and less punitive approach to crime than we practice today. Clarify this issue using our theories—and be sure to seek out the relevant facts as well. What are the key issues?

- Can you say more about the moral status of animals using our theories? What are the implications for food production, drug testing, pet-keeping, hunting, zoos?

- Ease of life today may impose immense costs on the future. When we waste scarce natural resources and litter the earth with non-biodegradable but cheap items, our descendants bear the burdens of compensation and clean-up. When we risk altering the climate, we risk imposing unknown but possibly immense costs on the future, too. The planner and futurist William McDonough calls this "intergenerational remote tyranny." What kinds of moral values is he invoking? Is he right? What others are relevant?

Still More Theories

Ethics continues to diversify. We may actually need more theories to speak to moral values newly emerging now. Consider the values of nature. Although there are ways to work the values of nature into, say, utilitarianism, by arguing that we should care about nature because in the long run it serves our own happiness, it is also clear (I hope) that nature is not valuable *just* for human happiness. And, while we may be able to glimpse a way to extend the ethics of persons, say, to some (or maybe all) other animals, it is certainly not clear how to extend it to rivers and mountains or the Earth itself.

Instead, environmental values may need to be recognized as (part of?) a new family of moral values—although of course there are many questions about just what kind of ethical theory might best give voice to this new family of values as well.

As a final exercise for this chapter, consider how you might spell out and justify the values of the natural world beyond the human sphere. How far can you make use of the three theories this chapter has introduced? When do you find yourself needing to go farther? In what direction? Why does nature matter so much?

NOTES

Classic texts introduced in this chapter are John Stuart Mill's *Utilitarianism*; Martin Buber's *I and Thou*; Immanuel Kant's *Grounding for* [or *Foundations of*] *the Metaphysics of Morals*; and Aristotle's *Nichomachean Ethics* (sometimes just titled *Ethics*), all available in multiple editions. Aristotle is cited from Book I, 1097b23–1098a19 in the W. D. Ross translation from Oxford University Press (New York/Oxford: 2009). Excerpts from all of these books, along with other classic and contemporary texts in ethics, can also be found in many anthologies and on line. One especially good mix of classic readings and sharply argued applications is Steven Cahn, editor, *Exploring Ethics: An Introductory Anthology* (New York/Oxford: Oxford University Press, 2008). The "Ethics Updates" website at http://ethics.sandiego.edu/ offers detailed resources on each type of ethical theory, along with their critics, and some consideration of new types of ethical theories as well.

4

WHEN VALUES CLASH

~

Mention the word "ethics" today and all too quickly we think of controversies. Abortion, Affirmative action, Animal rights, Assisted suicide ... and that's just the A's. For many people, conflict seems to be the main subject of ethics itself.

Moral values certainly *differ*, in all sorts of interesting and deep ways. Still, difference is not necessarily the same as *conflict*. Differing values may just as readily complement each other. Moreover, when moral differences do pose problems, there may also be quite natural and ready ways to resolve them. There may even be inspiring ways to move past those problems altogether. Could it be that we need a much more constructive toolbox when we take up moral controversies and disagreements?

RIGHT VERSUS RIGHT

Today we learn to interpret most moral differences as deeply polarized and probably irresolvable oppositions. Moral differences are quickly turned into the most painful and useless sorts of conflicts: fundamental, sharp clashes with no common ground to be found and no way to make progress together. Even TV news programs now feature opinionated and loud arguments between radically opposed positions, a lot more heat than light. We know all too well that in popular moral debates, the loudest advocates usually act as if only one side can be right, that only one side—their own, of course—has a monopoly on truth and the other side is just misguided or blind or even evil.

This is "either/or" thinking. *Either* one side is right *or* the other is right. No ambiguity, no gray areas, no middle ground. No other possibilities get discussed or even imagined. The approach is adversarial, win–lose, winner-take-all. And it is so common and familiar that sometimes it seems to be the only possible way of understanding or carrying on disagreements. No wonder my students come to ethics courses expecting a fight.

Yet there is another way—and a far more promising one. Shift focus just a little, and what come into view are more complex values, many of them shared, and not simply in opposition—very different than the contending simplistic extremes we are usually offered.

Take the abortion debate. As we know all too well, it very often reduces to shouting "Life!" on the one side and "Choice!" on the other, as if the question can only be an either/or. But here is a surprising but still totally obvious observation: all of us value both Life *and* Choice. Every one of us is pro-life. Life is what makes love and community and beauty and everything else possible. Those acts associated with creating and preserving and honoring life—sex, childbirth, nurturing a baby, caring for the sick, mourning the dead—are among the most profound of life's experiences.

Just as clearly, though, every one of us is pro-choice. Freedom, self-determination, the right to control what happens to our own bodies—this is absolutely basic, too. In politics, in the stores, in "lifestyle"—choice is everything. Some people even think that seat belts or smoking bans are unjustified limits on physical freedom—the most trivial of restrictions compared to pregnancy and childbirth.

We have *two* sets of basic values here—not just one "right" one. Both are essential. Rather than "the other side," whichever it is, being misguided or immoral or barely even comprehensible, the actual truth is that we pretty much agree with them. It is not an either/or. *Both* Life *and* Choice matter, and matter deeply.

Of course, deep differences still remain. Facing actual abortion decisions, when hard choices must be made, we may prioritize the shared basic values differently. Still, it pays to remember that those values themselves may well be shared. Many pro-choice advocates are actually quite conflicted about abortion—they feel the loss, too—and might not choose it for themselves but think it at least needs to be an option for others in more desperate straits. It is a sad commentary on the state of the debate at present that this surprises people on the pro-life side. Similarly, not all pro-life advocates oppose abortion in all cases. Most are willing to accept abortion in cases where the pregnant woman was raped or when her life is in danger, a position that may not be totally consistent with the single value of fetal life—a criticism sometimes raised by harder-liners—but is in fact a recognition, and surely a welcome recognition, that there can be other basic values at stake, too.

Again, it is a sad commentary on the state of the debate at present that these areas of overlap and relative agreement are not recognized or honored. Could it not be *our* job to do better?

Assisted Suicide

Consider the question of assisted suicide. Here the debate is about whether doctors should be allowed to assist certain people to enable their own dying—people who are approaching death or total disability and are often in great pain. One side says Yes: death may be the only way in which some people can finally escape unrelenting pain or degradation; besides, we are free individuals entitled to make that choice to end our own lives. Is it so much more to request help in dying?

But the other side recoils. Allowing and perhaps encouraging doctors to assist a person to die, even if only when asked, takes a step toward devaluing life, and who knows where it will lead? Life is infinitely precious even in pain, and medicine above all professions needs to stay true to it.

It is another tough question. Once again, though, it is a tough question precisely because both answers have valid points. Freedom from pain matters, *and* autonomy matters, *and* respect for life matters. We do have a problem here. But the real problem is not that we somehow irresolvably disagree about basic values. We agree all too well—about all too *many*.

Ethical theories weigh in on assisted suicide, too, also in the name of more than one basic value. Utilitarians stress that one good reason in favor of assisted suicide is the relief of pain. The prevention or relief of pointless suffering is a good thing. Listen to the stories of some of the people who want and need help to die, and your heart goes out to them. Let them go!

But there are other values in play too. Character matters in the face of suffering and death. We can respond with courage, humility, resoluteness—virtues. We are called to care and responsiveness in the face of others' suffering as well—virtues, too.

Kant proposes a striking way to think about suicide. "If [we] kill [ourselves] in order to escape from painful circumstances," he wrote, "we use a person [ourselves] merely as a means to maintain a tolerable condition to the conclusion of life." Once life offers us no more pleasure, we conclude that our life has no more value. But this move, so very natural if you think mainly in terms of pleasures and pains, is for Kant to overlook a whole dimension of value. Our lives, he argues, matter *in themselves*, not just as a means to something else, even of our own. We must respect our own lives just as we must respect the lives of others around us.

What Is Each Side Right About?

Here, too, we do not really have a conflict between right and *wrong*. We have a conflict between right and *right*. "Only dogmatism," wrote the twentieth-century pragmatic philosopher John Dewey,

> can suppose that serious moral conflict is between something clearly bad and something known to be good, and that uncertainty lies wholly in the will of the one choosing. Most conflicts of importance are conflicts between

things which are or have been satisfying, not between good and evil.

That is, most moral conflicts are real, not just confusions or mistakes by one side about what really matters. It is not a question of "either/or" but of "both/and."

We therefore can—in fact, we therefore *must*—engage moral conflicts in a very different spirit. Instead of approaching opposing views looking for their weak points (according to us) or asking what is wrong with the morals of the people on the "other side," we can start the other way around. We can look for their strong points. Ask not which side is right, but what *each* side is right *about*. The real task then is to clarify the issue: to take adequate account of all the important values that are at stake.

I do *not* mean that *all* contending views must be right about something. We are not about to acknowledge the values of Nazis or slave-owners or people who care not a whit what kind of moral wreckage they leave in their wake. Values like theirs need to be judged against the basic values that ethics aims to speak for—remember, the basic needs and legitimate expectations of others as well as yourself—and will be found wanting. To have a genuine voice in moral debates you need to be working from genuine moral values. *Then* we try to work it out.

Still, again, in many important moral debates, each side really does bring genuine moral values to the table. Usually the harder challenge is recognizing the moral seriousness of other sides' views, not their moral shortcomings. But to understand ourselves and others as trying to live up to many sorts of moral values already paints a very different picture of "conflict" than a head-on collision between polarized and irreconcilable points of view. Is it not more like a shared challenge to take up *together?*

FINDING THE BEST BALANCE

We may hesitate to acknowledge "right" on more than one side in moral debates because we fear that then we will be unable to decide anything. If both sides are somehow right, what can we *do*? If opposed moral values or ethical theories bear on the issue, and in different ways, how do we sort it all out? How can we possibly resolve practical moral questions and move ahead?

Constructive Problem-solving

The answer is actually quite simple, and no surprise at all. It is to try to find the best *balance* between the various values at stake. Work to find the choices that answer to as many of the relevant values as fully as we can. Try to take account of the values on all sides. More strategically, look beneath and around the sorest points of contention to find ways that the underlying values and interests can be co-achieved, even when at first or on the surface they may seem to be mutually exclusive. And when not all of our values are fully achievable, we can at least try to figure out the next best options, ways in which we can still do reasonably well, even if not perfectly, by all of them.

Currently I commute about thirty-five miles each way to the university where I teach. I'd much prefer to be able to walk or bike, for all sorts of reasons. Ecologically, it would relieve the world of one car and its pollution. Personally, it would save me time and give more pleasure. Physically, it would be healthier. The wish to be closer to my work for these reasons could conceivably lead me to change jobs, or move.

At the same time, though, there are many other values served by things the way they are. My university is an excellent fit, I am lucky to be able to do good work there, and there is loyalty and affection both ways. My family is well established in our home city, and both I and my partner and children have found special communities (and schools and jobs) that we would not have if we were to move (or it would mean more driving for everyone else). Meantime I compensate in other ways, such as driving a super-low-emissions car (alas, there is no train or bus) and using the commute time as productively as I can.

Thus, trying to make the most responsible *overall* choice, I end up on the road. It's certainly not perfect, but it is also, surely, a reasonable way to put everything together, and for the time being it may be the best I can do. That is how life goes.

The same kind of balancing and adjustment can work even for the most conflicted moral issues. Take the assisted suicide debate again. As we have seen, different moral values pull us in different directions, and they are not all compatible. Yet there are still quite reasonable ways to acknowledge all of the relevant values and concerns and make progress together. My experience in many discussions of assisted suicide over the years is that many people on both sides would be willing to accept a policy that allowed assisted suicide in such cases but under tightly controlled conditions. Several independent doctors would have to concur; waiting periods could be required; double- and triple-checks would be necessary to be sure patients were not just temporarily depressed; communities and governments would need to be sure that people in pain always have alternatives—but *then*, given all this, if people still resolutely seek to die, we need to respect their wishes.

It may be possible, in short, to legalize assisted suicide in a limited way that both acknowledges the seriousness of taking life and its social dangers while also recognizing that, sometimes at least, it can be a humane and proper choice, even another way of respecting life itself. You might be interested to know that just this kind of policy has been adopted in the state of Oregon—and repeatedly reaffirmed by the voters—with results that are certainly not an epidemic of suicides. About fifty people per year have secured permission to request assisted suicide in recent years. Again, this kind of policy is probably not morally perfect, but it is also, surely, a reasonable way to put everything together, and for the time being it may be the best we can do. That is how life goes!

The Problem-solving Mindset

Balancing, adjusting, seeking maximally inclusive solutions—all of this is a familiar process. We do the same sort of thing, only with less fanfare or bother, when we make joint decisions with family or friends or teammates, or when legislators try to craft bills to garner the support of a majority, or in innumerable other practical settings where many different desires or interests or values are involved and none of them automatically rules the day. These problems do not call for a legalistic or judgmental approach, intent on one and only one specific desire or interest or value entirely winning out, but rather for a *problem-solver's mindset*, intent on all sides getting as much as possible of what they want or value.

The problem-solver's mindset has an ethic as well—and surely an appealing one. When you begin by recognizing that all the sides in a debate probably share many of the relevant values—when you acknowledge that there actually is right on other sides—then those other sides no longer seem quite so "other" in the first place. The problem-solver's mindset opens up the possibility that in a certain sense we stand on the *same* side, even with our differences. Rather than fighting each other, then, we can take up the shared challenge together. After all, as Roger Fisher and William Ury put it in their influential book *Getting to Yes*, it's not really the other side that's the problem; it's the *problem* that's the problem. That is the problem-solving mindset in a nutshell: not an attempt to win, not to beat (down) someone else, but to work it out.

Problem-solvers also learn to listen beneath polarized standpoints for values and interests that, even though different, may be compatible. Fisher and Ury call this focusing on *interests* rather than on *positions*. "Positions"—our official, simplified stances—may sharply diverge and often seem non-negotiable. They're meant to. Sometimes we may lock ourselves into such positions because we expect that they are the only possible way to think morally, or to stick up for what we take to be the basic value at stake, or the only way just to be heard. But underneath, still, our actual values and interests may not be incompatible at all.

For instance, I have tried to show that both sides in the abortion debate value quite similar things—and hold more than one basic value. As we know all too well, each side has been hardened and simplified into a one-value (now actually one-*word*) "position" whose whole point, it seems, is to deny and put down the other. But this is partly because the supposedly essential positions concern exactly one question: whether, or how far, abortion is to be legally permitted. Look at the issue more broadly, and there are many other questions on which the two sides do not diverge but, believe it or not, actually *converge.*

The "pro-life" side does not just want abortion illegal. The "pro-choice" side does not just want abortion legal. What both actually want—along with the overwhelming majority of the American people, for as long as pollsters have asked the question—is less abortion. No one favors abortion per se (despite the label "pro-abortion," which is misleading precisely because it obscures this underlying agreement). We *all* would welcome a dramatic decrease in the demand or perceived need for abortion in the first place: that is, a dramatic reduction in the rate of unintended, unwanted pregnancies and the desperation with which some women therefore feel they need to seek abortion.

The two sides come to this conclusion for somewhat different reasons. For the pro-life side, it is mainly because reducing unintended, unwanted pregnancies would dramatically reduce the killing of fetuses, which they see as the moral equivalent of killing a born person. For the pro-choice side, it is mainly because reducing unintended, unwanted pregnancies would make "choice" more real. Women would be more in control of their own fertility and lives. Whichever the reasons, though, the key thing is that both sides could readily embrace very similar policy goals. We can seek to reduce unwanted pregnancies through a variety of means, like reducing sexual coercion and the social and cultural disempowerment of women; making pregnancies at the "wrong time" less of a stigma and making adoption much more accessible; and better access to effective birth control and at least some basic sex education. Some of these policies are controversial, too, of course, but they are still a great deal more amenable to real progress, mutual understanding, and cooperation.

In fact, it has already happened. The two sides have already worked together (I did say that: they have *worked together*) at times. When the welfare laws were up for revision in 1996, a group of powerful legislators proposed to deny assistance to children born of mothers under 18 or currently on welfare or whose paternity had not been established. In response a remarkable thing happened. Nearly all major organizations on both sides of the abortion issue came out against the proposal, including the National Right to Life Committee, Planned Parenthood, the U.S. Catholic Conference, and the National Organization of Women. Both sides feared that the results would be to coerce abortions among poor women. Both sides made the connections back to economic conditions. Pro-choice and pro-life organizations in fact jointly designed a comprehensive child-support reform plan as an alternative.

Again, it is not that they agreed with each other, point for point, about why abortion is a bad thing—although they certainly can agree in large part, as I've tried to show, since each side largely shares the other's values, too. Still, again, the key point is that more than one set of basic values can still be honored at the same time. Different sides' interests may converge on many day-to-day policies, and if we work from those convergences, ideally, our divergences may matter less in the long run. They will still be there—for sure—but they need not block us from mutual acknowledgment and enthusiastically going on together. Remember again: it is the *problem* that's the problem, not the people on the "other side." Or their values—which are quite likely, one way or the other, our values, too.

MORAL VISION

Finding the best balance is a head-on way of making progress in pressing moral debates, right now—for often we do need to be able to move ahead, as soon as we can, with practical measures. But there is also another and more ambitious way to move beyond clashes of values and to dramatically recast them.

Ethics at its best is not just *against* the problems of the moment or a debate over the least bad option. It can also be emphatically, visibly, clear-headedly *for* something, and something that is worked out, widely compelling, even beautiful. This we can call *Moral Vision*.

From Push to Pull

Moral values can push us toward some sort of moral minimum, morally getting by. Pushes, though, are generally not so welcome or so motivating. No one likes to be nagged or constantly reminded of their failings. We do not like getting pushed.

But a *pull* is also possible. Here the psychology is just the opposite. We are drawn toward something: it captivates us, it rouses the heart and the mind. We move not wearily or out of accommodation but out of real inspiration. In ethics, that kind of pull comes from making possibilities explicit: by laying out a moral vision.

Fundamentally, a moral vision is a positive and appealing longer-term alternative, beyond just meeting the needs of the moment and doing the best we can with an immediate, difficult situation. Visions look forward to a future where we can make a more complete resolution—perhaps in quite a different way than any of the currently available short-term options. We can co-design a future in which the current problems have been at least partly resolved, not by one side finally triumphing over the other side but by working out unexpected and ambitious ways to honor our basic shared values, and perhaps to deepen and develop more. We lift our eyes from the immediacy of conflict to look at larger and longer-term themes, with more space for possibility evident in the far-sightedness of the perspective. It is not that we necessarily eliminate the problems in front of us—we may still disagree there—but we may, all the same, find ways of enthusiastically and wholeheartedly going forward together.

Moral Vision at Work

Something very interesting happened when some of my students took up the assisted suicide issue for a class report a few years ago. They found a website that included biographies of the people that Dr. Jack Kevorkian—the (in)famous freelance crusader for assisted suicide—had helped to die. It was a pro-Kevorkian website. But we began to realize, as we read people's stories, that Kevorkian became a last resort for many people because they not only were in pain but also lacked any kind of family or social support. In some cases, their spouses or children were driven away by their very desperateness and need. In at least one case, this absence meant in turn that the affected person could not take strong painkillers, since he had no one to look after him, as medically required, when he was partly "knocked out."

We began to see, in short, that pain is not always the main issue. People who seek assisted suicide may not always be suffering physically. Instead the suffering may be emotional: they feel helpless, useless, and abandoned.

But neither side in the current debate would say that in this kind of case the right "answer" is death. Both would agree that the real answer is to create communities of care such that people are not abandoned in this way. It is not a question of the legality of assisted suicide at all. We need to *change focus*—toward a positive and in fact eminently shareable moral vision.

It doesn't follow that no one would ever request assisted suicide. Very real physical pain remains for some. We still have to figure out what the law should or shouldn't allow. The essential thing, though, is that the curtain now goes up on something much bigger and more hopeful: a society, finally, in which the old and the suffering are not abandoned and pushed to the side. That's a challenge to all of us, too, not just to stand by and judge the morality of certain kinds of suicide but to keep people from the kinds of losses that drive them to such desperation in the first place. Not just to formally affirm the personhood of the old and the suffering but to make it *concretely real*, celebrated, and practiced. What could be more visionary than that?

Or consider the death penalty debate—another case, I am afraid, of a debate preoccupied with after-the-fact, "positional" responses rather than looking to underlying causes and shareable, forward-looking visions. Whether a few dozen killers are executed or imprisoned for life— which is, in the end, the entire practical question about the death penalty—actually makes next to no difference to the understaffed, overcrowded, violent schools for crime and brutalization that the prisons have become for millions of inmates, not to mention the almost total inattention to victims' needs or to healing the rupture in community caused by crime. The whole system is a disaster, and we are fighting about a few extreme cases.

Again, arguably, what we really need is a bigger and shareable moral vision. For starters, we must begin to envision and build neighborhoods and workplaces where people really watch out for each other. We can undertake a restorative approach to justice, already under way in some places, that attends to the victims' and the community's losses when crime occurs. And then, going to the bottom of things, we must begin to build economies that offer ambitious or desperate young people better work than drug-peddling or burglary, schools that really prepare them for such work, and, indeed, a society that welcomes rather than rejects them.

This vision is morally committed, for sure, but it is not seriously controversial. Liberals and conservatives alike can embrace it. There are different routes to it that we no doubt will struggle over politically. But how much better such a world would be for *all* of us than crime- and fear-ridden lives! We can fight each other about how terminally to punish the worst offenders, or we can work together to try to make the world a better place, reducing the number and scale of those offenses along the way. It's up to us—which is it to be?

I do not mean, of course, that better neighborhoods, schools, and the like will somehow eliminate serious crimes. As with assisted suicide, people can and no doubt will still debate about the exactly most moral form of punishment. It remains a real question. But the turn toward vision does give us a shareable and actually hopeful way to speak to issues of security and crime generally—again, to widen the lens, and to take up the more fundamental, less divisive issues. Once again, it calls us to something potentially far more engaging and productive—together.

A Master Visionary

August 28, 1963. A quarter of a million people gathered at the Lincoln Memorial in Washington, D.C., for a rally for civil rights—the largest demonstration until then in American history—and in particular to support the Kennedy Administration's Civil Rights Bill. It was a fractious, bitter moment, and many feared that violence would mar the march. It did not. Overwhelmingly what we now remember from that day is Martin Luther King's great speech, "I Have a Dream."

But here is a remarkable thing. When King walked up to the microphone that day, there was nothing about a Dream in his speech. All he had written was a formal recitation of wrongs against black people. He finished it and was about to sit down—his time was up. But suddenly, the story goes, the gospel singer Mahalia Jackson, also on stage, called out, "Tell them about your *dream*, Martin! Tell them about the dream!" Other listeners shouted encouragement, too. And so, on the spot, King launched into an impassioned improvisation that made that speech into one of the shining moments of the century.

King gave the country a positive moral vision, an ideal framed not as a set of complaints or a preoccupation with the immediate flashpoints but in terms of long-term, shareable hopes—a collective way past the conflicts of the moment, an explicit and open invitation to a wary nation to join in the spirit of mutuality and cross-racial respect that the march, and the marchers right before him, themselves embodied.

I have a dream that one day on the red hills of Georgia the sons of former slaves and the sons of former slave owners will be able to sit down together at the table of brotherhood.

I have a dream that one day even the state of Mississippi, a state sweltering with the heat of injustice, sweltering with the heat of oppression, will be transformed into an oasis of freedom and justice.

I have a dream that my four little children will one day live in a nation where they will not be judged by the color of their skin but by the content of their character. I have a dream today ...

It could have been argued—in fact it *was* argued, all the time, by the "realists"—that King's Dreaming was a luxury. But who would remember King's speech today if he had put all the same points negatively?

> I have a *nightmare* that one day on the red hills of Georgia the sons of former slaves and the sons of former slave owners will *never* be able to sit down together at the table of brotherhood.
>
> I have a *nightmare* that ... the state of Mississippi, a state sweltering with the heat of injustice, sweltering with the heat of oppression, will be *never* transformed into an oasis of freedom and justice...

These are exactly the same points, yet the entire tone is reversed. It is only a negative moral vision, something to avoid. The feeling is unwelcome. We turn away in revulsion. We might go forward still, but unhappily, always looking backward in guilt and fear. King, by contrast, invited us to something wonderful, a way *forward* with hope.

King also invoked core American values. Literally in the very shadow of Lincoln, King spoke of the Emancipation Proclamation as a kind of "promissory note" that the nation had not yet paid. Yet he fully expected that it would be paid, and freely and gladly, too, once Americans recognized the moral need. That was the Dream, too, and that was what people so needed to hear, especially at that moment, with tensions rising across the South and the whole world watching: a dream of genuine equality, a better way for everyone, an appeal to the best in all of us. You could argue that it is really only a vivid description of what morality itself asks of us, community with all others without prejudice. Children, and all of us, judged by who we are and not by external characteristics.

Now that King's speech is so famous, the rhetoric of a "dream" has gotten rather, well, dreamy, and people invoke it for any kind of gauzy fantasy, almost as if vision were enough by itself. Of course, it is not. Not everyone, even now, shares King's vision of racial harmony; meanwhile King's own dreaming was to venture much further as he continued to change and grow. A few years later he turned against the Vietnam War and linked it directly to American materialism and self-indulgence. He dreamt of an America at peace with the rest of the world, especially peoples all around the globe who are different from us culturally and ethnically.

Real work remains. Real work always remains. Still, it is partly a measure of King's visionary genius, as well as his rhetorical genius, that we have come to share as much of his moral vision as we do already. And, of course, the dream lives on.

CONSTRUCTIVE STRATEGIES AT A GLANCE

- When genuine moral values are contending, ask not which side is right but *what each side is right about.*
- Seek the *best balance between the contending values*—decisions that take the best possible account of all the important values at stake.
- Build on the *shared and convergent interests* beneath apparently opposite and mutually exclusive "positions."
- Beyond the immediate conflict, work out *compelling and inclusive moral visions* that invite us all toward a better future.

FOR PRACTICE

Review

Summarize and review the main points of this chapter. What is the difference between an "either/or" and a "both/and" approach to moral conflicts? How could both sides be right? (Mostly?) How do we find the best balance between a large set of different and often seemingly opposed values? What is a "problem-solver's mindset"?

Why do moral visions "pull" rather than "push" us—and why does it matter? Can you think of your own most compelling examples of a moral vision?

What Do We Think?

In a genuine moral dispute, I have said, each side is right about something. Given our usual habits, though, it is a hard message to get. We're too used to debating polarized issues in the either/or mode. Just the mere acknowledgment that other sides have some points needs a lot of practice.

So practice. Begin by identifying your position on some hot-button issues, such as the death penalty, eating animals, drugs (hint: take some time to define your terms here), affirmative action (ditto), gay marriage, welfare (that is, how should society respond to the needs of the down-and-out?), and/or stricter environmental protection. Now, for each, consider the opposite position—the other side or sides. Ask yourself what the other side(s) are right about—not wrong, but right. Where do you actually agree with them? What are their strongest and most important points?

Of course you do not agree with their conclusions, or most of them, but it's very likely that you can still find shared or at least compatible values. I would be willing to bet that you share *most* of the other side's values, in fact, although you may give them somewhat different priorities. Write them down.

Thinking about the death penalty, for example, shared or compatible values might include *life* (both sides insist that life is precious, which is why murder is considered by both to be so heinous a crime and why the "pro" side thinks murderers deserve death, but it is also why the "anti" side thinks that execution only doubles the crime); *appropriate punishment* (since both sides condemn murder, both propose "ultimate punishments," execution or life in prison);

deterrence (preventing future crimes and murders); and *fairness* (convictions must be fair; the execution of innocent people and racially tainted verdicts are wrong).

Remember that your challenge here is not just to describe the other side's view. It's tempting to answer by just summarizing what you think they think. "They think this; they think that." That's helpful too, but the task here is to go much farther. Find the shared values. What do they think that you think too? What do you think they're right about? Go beyond "I think ..." and "They think ..." to "*We* think..." (Like this: *We* think that life matters. *We* think that punishment should fit the crime. *We* value a sense of security ... .)

Finally, ask how you can build on the values you have identified. Start looking for ways to balance them, or moral visions that might unite us beyond the pressing practical issues of the moment. Given the extensive areas of agreement about punishment and value of life just sketched, for example, how might you use the tools introduced in this chapter to develop a more widely agreeable and even inspiring approach to the punishment of murderers? Are there creative options, for example—alternatives besides either execution or life imprisonment? (You might need the next chapter to help you find them.)

You might also make a class project of going much further with the abortion issue in particular. This chapter makes a beginning— can you go further? What might a worked-out and shareable moral vision look like in this case? Is it actually so hard to figure out?

The Work Goes On

Concerned about the increasingly polarized character of our moral and political debates, a variety of organizations have sprung up in defense of dialogue and civic discourse and to promote a problem-solving approach to contentious moral and social issues. Below are a few. It's hard, useful, inspiring, sometimes amazing work. See what is going on, and, if it moves you, join in.

- Search for Common Ground: www.sfcg.org
- The Public Conversations Project: www.publicconversations.org

- National Coalition Building Institute: www.ncbi.org
- The National Coalition for Dialogue and Deliberation: http://www.thataway.org/

NOTES

The quote from John Dewey is from his essay "The Construction of Good," Chapter 10 of his book *The Quest for Certainty*, reprinted in James Gouinlock, *The Moral Writings of John Dewey* (New York: Hafner-Macmillan, 1976), Chapter 5, where the quotation can be found on p. 154.

For more details on "finding the best balance" in moral controversies, see my book *Toward Better Problems* (Philadelphia: Temple University Press, 1992), as well as *A 21st Century Ethical Toolbox*, Chapters 14 ("When Values Clash") and 17 ("Moral Vision"). Most of the websites just cited also include "how-to" pages and other useful links for promoting dialogue and constructive moral problem-solving. Fisher and Ury's classic book *Getting to Yes* (New York: Penguin, 1983) is essential reading on (as their subtitle puts it) "negotiating agreement without giving in." Students of philosophy might also consult Martin Benjamin's rigorously argued book *Splitting the Difference: Compromise and Integrity in Ethics and Politics* (Lawrence, KS: University Press of Kansas, 1990).

5

CREATIVE PROBLEM-SOLVING IN ETHICS

Creative thinkers generate new ideas and solutions to tough problems. Creativity in this sense is as essential in ethics as it is in practical problem-solving generally.

CREATIVITY AND THE ESSENCE OF ETHICS

A problem:

> A child in second grade underwent chemotherapy for leukemia. When she returned to school, she wore a scarf to hide the fact that she had lost all her hair. But some of the children pulled it off, and in their nervousness laughed and made fun of her. The child was mortified and that

afternoon begged her parents not to make her go back to school. Her parents tried to encourage her, saying, "The other children will get used to it, and anyway your hair will soon grow in again."

Say you were this class's teacher. Ethics surely requires you to defend the afflicted child. You can defend her with more or less skill, but the fact is (so it seems) that you need to read the class the Riot Act. This is a time when even young children must take some responsibility, to avoid causing hurt. Second grade is not too early to learn the lesson.

Honestly, though, you can predict what the effects will be. A few children get it, maybe. More are just going to "really feel sorry" for the poor kid, making both her and themselves terribly self-conscious. Others will retreat into sullenness. A few will put on a show of care but keep on taunting her behind your back. And she herself will be even more embarrassed and hurt.

These are not the results you want either. But is there any other way? Think about it. Really, what would *you* do?

The next morning, when their teacher walked into class, all the children were sitting in their seats, some still tittering about the girl who had no hair, while she shrank into her chair. "Good morning, children," the teacher said, smiling warmly in her familiar way of greeting them. She took off her coat and scarf. Her head was completely bald.

After that, a rash of children begged their parents to let them cut their hair. And whenever a child came to class with short hair, newly bobbed, all the children laughed merrily, not out of fear but out of the joy of the game. And everybody's hair grew back at the same time.

How wonderful—and how ethical! This teacher did something memorable and transformative, and morally far more powerful than a lecture ever could be. By shaving her own head, she invited her class into an entirely new way of relating to the child with no hair. She showed them that there is something to do besides gape at her or feel sorry for her. The bald child was no longer a problem or an object of pity, but a playmate with options, just like she was before. Maybe even better.

What a creative teacher! Would that all our teachers were like her—would that we were like her ourselves. And in all seriousness: why not?

A Sense of Possibility

You begin to glimpse the possibilities for ethical problem-solving a little beyond—maybe *more* than a little beyond—what we usually see. For one thing, even the most seemingly "stuck" and readily moralized situation may have totally unexpected possibilities, ways out or beyond that are far outside the usual range of options we consider.

You also begin to see that ethical problem-solving need not be just a matter of fixing a specific problem. It may also be an occasion to better the world in a larger way. Think again of those children at the moment their teacher first takes off her scarf and they see her shaved head. Confusion might be their first reaction. Then, quickly, the dawning realization of what they are being invited to: a completely new way of relating not just to the bald student but to their teacher and finally to each other. A stronger sense of values, of ethical possibility, comes into play, and it expands to the whole class and everything it does.

The implications also go far beyond this one situation. Last year I had a student who shaved his head, along with all of his family members, in support of his mother who had lost her hair from chemotherapy. Whole city blocks have done it to buck up a stricken neighbor. Fighting cancer is partly a lonely battle, but there is far more that the rest of us can offer. Solidarity!

EXPANDING POSSIBILITIES

Creative problem-solving is the art of expanding possibility. There are a number of very practical methods for doing so, all of them already in use in a variety of practical fields, but as applicable in ethics as anywhere else.

Creative Explorations

The first task is just to generate more ideas. You can even treat it as a pure question of quantity. It is a helpful and eye-opening practice just to try to get, say, ten ideas on the table before thinking at all about which to choose.

One way is to deliberately *go asking* for new ideas. Something as simple as just talking to other people may readily lead us to whole new perspectives. What do your grandfather or your doctor think about assisted suicide? What do veterinarians or life long hunters or hard-core vegans know about other animals that might open up new perspectives and possibilities for you? Ask!

More formally, there is the method of *brainstorming.* Although we sometimes use the word "brainstorming" loosely for any kind of creative group process, it actually does have formal rules. The key rule is to defer criticism. It is tempting and safe to react to any new suggestion with doubts and obstacles. Brainstorming asks us to do just the opposite: to consider how some new idea *could* work, not why it probably wouldn't. Even a crude and obviously unrealistic idea, given some breathing room and passed around the room, may evolve into something much more realistic. Meanwhile, it may also spark other new ideas. (This is why another rule of brainstorming is to set a high numerical quota—say, twenty new ideas, however unrealistic they may seem—before any comparison or evaluation is allowed at all.) Let ideas hitchhike on each other.

Also, look to *other places and times.* How is it that some societies will not tolerate leaving even a single person homeless? That for native peoples in North America, the ramifications of any decision had to be worked out for seven generations? That in Japan, abortion is legal and common, while at the same time the loss of the fetus is recognized in Buddhist ceremonies and there are even graveyards for fetuses? (The Japanese also have ceremonies and graveyards for animals sacrificed to medical research—the sacrifices continue but they are acknowledged and regretted, too.) Surely we can learn from other societies' ways of dealing with issues like these, whether we want to move with them or not. They put our own practices in a wider and more suggestive light.

That's the key word: *suggestive.* Creativity asks us to be alert to new and unexpected perspectives and new ideas that may come along from all sorts of unexpected sources. In the last chapter, for example, we ended up rethinking the entire question of assisted suicide because of a few biographies my students found on the Internet—and those biographies were posted with quite a different intent than we drew from them.

Or again, we may begin to see new possibilities in the gay marriage debate when we realize how fluid marriage seems to be in general. The French worked out a new kind of "civil contract" as an alternative to traditional marriage meant for gay couples, but more than half of the takers have turned out to be straight. Meanwhile, some conservatives are promoting a kind of super-marriage that cannot be dissolved except in the most extreme cases. It seems that a lot of people are looking for alternatives to marriage as we have known it. To me it certainly sounds like an invitation to some serious creative thinking!

Creative Provocations

Walk too many times the same way and your path becomes a rut. The same is true of our thoughts. At first new ideas associate widely and flexibly, but soon they solidify, they form fixed and automatic patterns, and any other association becomes hard to even imagine. A more dramatic form of creativity is therefore needed to loosen our ideas: to rearrange them, to break out of fixed associations, to force us out of our ruts—even a little roughly, as need be. Our ideas may need to be "unsettled," both literally and in the sense that doing so may induce some discomfort. Take the discomfort as a sign that you are getting somewhere. And stay alert, once again, for suggestive new possibilities that arise.

For one thing, you can deliberately *reverse* certain features of the problem. For example, suppose that you are thinking about the question of animal dissection in schools: whether and under what conditions students with moral objections should be excused from animal dissection. Try "reversing" your ideas a little—just to see what happens, what new ideas might arise. Normally students dissect the specimen animal. One rough-cut reversal might therefore be: what if the *animal* dissected the *students?*

Quickly now—don't reject such a thought out of hand just because, practically speaking, it is absurd, even outrageous. Obviously we are not actually going to dissect people ... but mightn't this idea, taken as a kind of suggestion, open up some other interesting ideas, even just around the corner? (Remember, we *wanted* something at least a little wild for a genuinely new creative provocation.) For one thing, it might remind us that we can learn a lot just from looking carefully at our own or each other's bodies—about blood flow, for example, or muscles and leverage. So why not study our own bodies *live* rather than animals dead? Or we could study animals themselves live.

Already, then, you have a fresh angle on the whole dissection question—a quite practical new idea even from an outrageous starting-point. Why dissect dead animals at all? Mightn't there be better alternatives to dissection not just for students with moral reservations, but for everyone?

A related method is *exaggeration*. Take some aspect of the problem before you and make it as extreme, as overdone, as you can. Then, once again, stand back and see what new ideas or perspectives it might provoke. To exaggerate dissection, for example, you might visualize somehow literally going inside the animal. Not merely by methodically disassembling its remains with a knife in a lab but actually jumping inside its body.

Literally it is impossible, of course. Even the very idea may seem useless and irresponsible. But once again, hold on: couldn't we move from such a wild idea to something more workable? How about ... computer simulation? In fact, doesn't the computer open up all sorts of exciting new virtual possibilities, like shrinking yourself down to the size of a cell and touring a living body through the veins (or lymphatic system or bile ducts or...) or tracking changes in the body over time or in different activities (sleep, exercise, sex, alarm...)? What a thrill!

The very simplest and at the same time most radical of ways to reassociate ideas is what the problem-solving guru Edward De Bono calls the "random word method." We could also call it *inviting exotic associations.* Go to the dictionary, DeBono says, or to any book for that matter. Open the book to any page and pick out a word at random—any word will do. (Or listen in for two seconds to random conversations—I flip the car radio on and off for this if I am using this method while driving; or try to remember some fragment of a dreams; or... .) Then see what associations that word (or image, etc.) suggests. Immediately your thinking has a truly new stimulus. You are not just going around in the same old circles.

Thinking about the dissection issue one more time, for example, I happened to look at a pill bottle on the table—another kind of random or "exotic" prompt. At first I made no suggestive associations. Then I remembered reading recently that some doctors are using jellybean-sized "camera pills" to scan the stomach and intestines for tumors or infections. Next up are even smaller and remote-controlled versions that can also collect cell samples and administer medication. Soon we should be able to send them through the blood as well.

So why not expand the use of "camera pills" from medical diagnosis into the schools? We can explore our very own bodies, from the inside, as living laboratories. Classes can explore each other's stomachs, bad knees, you name it. Kids will love this! And dissection, with its stink of formaldehyde and moral queasiness, would be long gone.

You see, anyway, that ideas *can* be systematically reassociated—it is even *easy*—and that from the new and unfamiliar and sometimes even absurd-sounding combinations that result, genuinely fresh ideas can arise. We just imagined three different and exciting alternatives to dissection in the space of as many pages. You only need to give the process some time and approach your question with an open mind. Who knows what is possible until you try?

REFRAMING PROBLEMS

Sometimes, surprisingly enough, there are still more creative ways to address ethical problems. There actually may be better methods than "solving" our problems in the most straightforward way. You may change or recast the very problem itself. Here are three ways to try.

Revisit Outlying Parts of the Problem

Consider *all* the parts of a problem, not just the one or two that currently fill the screen. Each aspect can be reversed, varied, questioned. New possibilities will come up. It may well be that some other aspect of a problematic situation, pushed into the background at the moment, offers us a way to go forward while the current routes seem blocked.

Emmanuel Evans ran a department store during the 1940s and 1950s in my city, Durham, North Carolina. The store had an attached, sit-down cafeteria. Segregation-era laws forbade the seating of black people in such an eating establishment: they had to stand, get their food, and go outside to eat. Evans was unwilling to continue treating his black customers in this way. But what to do? The direct approach—seating black people in defiance of the law—would quickly end with nothing but fines and jail (this was before the Civil Rights era). Closing the cafeteria served no one's interests either.

So the direct approach was blocked. What about an indirect approach? Mightn't the problem yield to an approach from another angle? Naturally we first imagine changing things for the *black* customers. But suppose, Evans starting thinking, that things could be changed for the *white* customers instead? Couldn't white people (also) stand? Evans finally realized that he could just remove all the tables, so that no one was seated. No law was broken, but a powerful statement was made. His cafeteria became the first desegregated eating place in town. And Evans, by the way, later became one of Durham's best-loved mayors.

Problems as Opportunities

Another way to reframe problems is to take the problem before us not as a difficulty to be overcome or gotten rid of but as an actual opportunity to be welcomed. Instead of trying to solve the problem, we can ask instead how we can make *use* of it—not, or not just, as a "problem" but as a resource, as a solution, if we can just find the right problem for it, or reconceive the one in front of us.

This method itself—at least the automatic part—is very simple. Take any problem. Seek the very core of the difficulty. Identify it, state it clearly. Then ask yourself: Can I think of any way in which this "problem" might actually be welcomed? Are there opportunities in it? For what?

Case in point. Go to any "old-age home" and you will find people desperate for something constructive to do. There are some organized games and other activities, but still the feeling is that time is simply being filled. Professionals are even trained and hired to find ways to keep the occupants busy—disguising what we normally assume to be the simple fact that there really *is* nothing for them to do.

You could think of some creative responses in the usual problem-solving mode. Adapting computer games for older people? (A rather large market, you would think.) How about more crafts? These are fine ideas, but they are also still in the mode of solving the problem as it stands: filling up older adults' time. A seriously creative approach would be to ask what that unfilled time is an *opportunity* for. Is it really a problem, at all, we'd want to ask—or more like a *resource*?

Ask the question in this way and, right away, everything looks different. Of course it is a resource! Most older folks are not going to be blazing wilderness trails or driving delivery trucks or hanging sheet rock, but surely there are many ways that they can contribute. There may even be some ways in which *only* they can contribute. Here we have skilled, experienced, patient people, anxious for some constructive work. Why should it be hard to hook their abilities up with community needs?

Nursing homes could be connected with public libraries, for example, so the occupants could take over cataloguing and book care. It's good, careful, and quiet work—plus they'd have all the books and videos they want close at hand. Older adults could also take over or create community historical museums. In almost all tribal and traditional communities, the elders are the custodians of the community's history. They carry the memories and instruct the young. Why are we letting the elders and the history slip away?

Even better: we know that many young parents are desperate for good-quality childcare. Buildings are built—sometimes right next to the nursing home—where staff are once again hired and trained, this time to find ways to keep the children busy and maybe even teach them something. But why not bring the very young and the very old *together* in a setting in which both can help each other? The old can tell their stories to the very people who above all love stories. And the young can help tend to the needs of the old, learning something of life cycles and of service in the process.

Reframing problems in this way does take some imaginative work. Usually it will not be obvious at first how the seeming problem could possibly be an opportunity. It may seem silly even to ask. But you have seen already that it is the absurd or uncomfortable question that can sometimes be the most productive. Just ask anyway: "What *could* this 'problem' be an opportunity for?" Use the other tools from this chapter to help generate some concrete ideas. And stick with it!

Think Prevention

We understand the logic of prevention when it comes to health. Everyone knows that it's better to take vitamins and exercise than to wait until you get sick and then deal with the illness. We do not always act on this knowledge, for a variety of reasons, but we do know it.

In ethics the strategy could be the same. Look *before* or *behind* a problem as it is usually presented. Do not just take "the" problem for granted. Instead, consider whether it even needs to come up in the first place. Ask whether a few small changes, a few steps back, can change everything about the problem here and now, or perhaps even keep it from coming up at all. This is a third method for reframing problems.

It seems that when fertility clinics first started storing couples' fertilized embryos, they found themselves in huge battles when couples split up. Which partner "owned" the embryos? You could imagine a lot of ethical head-shaking and decades of contentious cases winding their ways through the courts. The clinics, wisely, quickly took a very different and preventive approach. Now, before they accept any embryos, they simply ask each couple to designate one or the other as the embryos' owner in the event of divorce. No more problem! The best solution was to prevent the contention from arising at all.

Or again: the best approach to the challenge of recycling may be to reduce or eliminate the need to recycle in the first place, especially by redesigning products and packaging so that they never become "junk" at all. "Precycling," it's called, rather than recycling. Make products that biodegrade rapidly, or have other attractive uses, building blocks maybe, or collectibles (why ever pass it on?), or toys (think of the marketing angles there), or even are edible themselves (drink the drink and then have the bottle for dessert). Or just require manufacturers to take them back, like the European Union already does—*then* we'll get reusable products in a hurry.

In any case, clearly there may be more and better ways to think about the ethically responsible use of materials than just to worry about how to get people to recycle more. In general, probably more often than we think, the *most* effective solution to a problem may be just to keep the problem itself from coming up. Creative problem-solving takes many forms!

Today you can hardly even mention the word "moral" without "dilemma" coming up in the next sentence, if it waits that long. *Moral dilemmas*, we say, and shake our heads, as if there is no other form that a moral issue might take.

Actually, though, a dilemma is a very special thing. Strictly speaking, a dilemma is a problem in which there are only two options, sharply opposed to each other, and both unappealing. Remember Sartre's young man in occupied Paris, introduced in Chapter 2? Either (says Sartre) he must abandon his mother to flee to England to fight the Nazis, or he must stay with her and abandon the struggle. Or consider the famous "Heinz dilemma," from the psychologist Lawrence Kohlberg's research on children's moral development:

> A woman was near death from cancer. One drug might save her, a form of radium that a druggist in the same town had discovered. The druggist was charging $2000, ten times what the drug cost him to make. The sick woman's husband, Heinz, went to everyone he knew to borrow the money, but he could only get together about half of what it cost. He told the druggist that his wife was dying and asked him to sell it cheaper or let him pay later. But the druggist said, "No." The husband got desperate and broke into the man's store to steal the drug for his wife. Should the husband have done that? Why?

It seems that Heinz can either steal the drug or watch his wife die. Again, there are supposed to be no other choices, and both of these have obvious ethical liabilities.

Equipped with a few creative problem-solving tools, though, we might want to question the assumption that all—or even many—practical moral issues are in fact dilemmas. How many alleged "dilemmas" might really be what logicians call "*false* dilemmas"? How many times, when we seem stuck, do we really just need some ready ways of generating new possibilities or reframing the problem itself?

I give the Heinz problem to my students after they have had some training in creative problem-solving. I do not tell them that for the last forty years or so it has been consider a classic example of an unsolvable dilemma. I just ask: can they think of any other options for poor old Heinz? It turns out that they can—easily. Here are a few of their suggestions.

For one thing, Heinz might offer the druggist something besides money. He may have some skill that the druggist could use. Maybe he's a good house painter or piano tuner or a skilled chemist himself. He could barter, trading the use of his skills for the drug.

Or suppose Heinz called a newspaper. Nothing like a little bad publicity to change the druggist's mind or to help the sick woman gain a few donations.

What about public or community assistance? Almost every society in which modern medicine is available has developed some systematic way of offering it to people who cannot afford it. As a last-ditch option, a group of health care advocates in one of my workshops even suggested that Heinz's wife steal the drug herself and get arrested for it, since most state laws require prisons to offer medical treatment to inmates!

And of course there is the question of health insurance. Why have they (apparently) none? Doesn't a system that creates intolerable conflicts like this need to be changed? Maybe the real problem is not just Heinz's but everyone's.

Closer in, there is the afflicted person's family and/or community. Think of the appeals you see in hardware stores and community groceries, complete with photographs, a town rallying to buy an afflicted kid a bone marrow transplant, another chance at life. Again, don't the rest of us need to get involved—why are we treating this just as *Heinz's* problem?

Finally, why is the druggist so inflexible? Maybe he needs the money to promote or keep on developing his drug. But in that case Heinz could argue that a spectacular cure would be the best promotion of all. Maybe his wife should get it free, or even get paid to participate in a drug test. At the least, Heinz could buy half the drug with the money he can raise, and then—if it works—ask for the rest to complete the demonstration.

There are more ideas still, but you get the picture. Heinz's situation is *not* truly a dilemma. He—and we—have other options, some of which, like public or community assistance, may actually bring the underlying and supposedly incompatible values into unexpected convergence.

I am sure that some moral problems really *are* dilemmas, especially when they need immediate answers and reframing and preventive strategies are harder to apply. And they may be redescribed (or new ones invented) if the aim is to preserve some telling conflict of values "in theory." The stark story they tell may be useful for some purposes.

At the same time, however, the starkness of such stories may mislead us about what moral problems are more typically like. Are dilemmas in fact the natural form in which actual, practical moral problems come to us? From the point of view of creativity, at least, I believe that we would be much wiser to start with the opposite assumption: that we live in a much more open world, a world in which ethical problems, like most of life's challenges, invite us into a broader field of practical possibility. Welcome and make use of it!

FOR PRACTICE

Review

Summarize the main points of this chapter. What is creativity – in general, and specifically in ethics? What is the difference between expanding options and reframing problems? Review the specific methods introduced in this chapter and give an example for each.

CREATIVE PROBLEM-SOLVING STRATEGIES AT A GLANCE

To expand your options:

- Explore the problem by *asking around, brainstorming,* and *looking to other places and times.*
- Rearrange your ideas, break fixed associations, by *reversing* or *exaggerating* the elements of the problem and *inviting exotic associations.*

To reframe problems:

- *Revisit outlying parts of the problem.*
- Are there ways that the *problem might be an opportunity?* (for what?)
- *Think prevention* (can we prevent the problem from even coming up, or from coming up in so difficult a form?).

Challenges

Here are some ethical questions and issues to take up in a creative spirit. Use all of the tools in this chapter. Stick with them long enough to give them a chance to work. And don't settle for new ideas that are only a little bit different but basically just ring a few changes on something familiar. The methods in this chapter can take you much further than that!

- Does Sartre's young man really have no other options besides the two simple and sharply opposed alternatives that he is torn between? No ways, for example, to contribute to the war effort *and* stay with his mother? Sartre tells him that the need to "just choose" in such drastic situations is part of the human condition. Is this good advice?

- This chapter hinted that it may be possible to rethink marriage in creative ways—indeed, it is already beginning to happen. Can you devise any creative improvements? Mightn't there be new forms of intimate partnership that could be better than marriage as we've known it? Such as?

- We're told that there is a dilemma between birth mothers' rights to privacy and adoptees' rights to "know where they came from." Maybe so. But maybe not. We won't really know until we look at actual evidence. Some states, for example, allow adoptees to find out who was their birth mother. Others have established a registry so that those birth mothers and adoptees who wish to be found can be put in contact with each other. How have these and other arrangements worked? What would be some creative further experiments?

- The average age of first sexual intercourse is under 16 years for American teens, the lowest age of any major industrialized countries. It seems a bit young. (Is it? Why?) The United States also has a much higher teen pregnancy rate than most other industrialized nations and vastly higher rates of sexually transmitted disease. Are there any ways to change our angle here? (One hint: Why does "sexually active" have to mean exactly one form of sexual activity? Isn't that just a bit, well, unimaginative? And why should "abstinence" be the only alternative?)

- Especially in rough economic times, large numbers of people fall into poverty and need some kind of help, at least for a short time. On the other hand, dependency and abuse are worries regarding the welfare system as we have known it. How else might welfare systems be organized?

- We also struggle with how to respond to people asking for money in the streets. We want to help but have also learned to wonder what the money is really going for. Some of us give a dollar anyway—how can you turn away? Others make it a policy to refuse. Couldn't there be some different and more creative ways of meeting this situation? (Hint: What if what's given is not money?)

- People who disagree profoundly with important political and social decisions need some way to visibly register their disagreement and attempt to sway others to their point of view—in short, to protest. But what is the best form for such protest? Too many of the current forms of protest are so obviously pushed into invisibility or irrelevance that the protestors become embittered and cynical—or turn to violence. With several classmates who hold different political perspectives, use the tools in this chapter to invent three morally healthier and more constructive forms of protest.

Why Wait for Problems?

A further step. Look around for institutions or practices that are not currently ethical problems and consider how you might creatively improve them in ethical directions. For example: we have Mother's Day and Father's Day and maybe Grandparents' Day, but mostly these are occasions for sending a card or maybe going on a shopping trip. Why not ask: How can we better celebrate our forebears—more fully, more meaningfully, more consistently? Then, too, what about Children's Day? And who else aren't we celebrating enough?

Another approach: Look for places where ethics has been notably successful, and then ask whether the same successes can be generalized to other areas. Find solutions first, so to speak, and then search for suitable problems. For example, I have mentioned families or neighbors who have shaved their own heads to support someone who has lost their hair to chemotherapy. We have the general idea. But are there other and far more powerful ways, both practical and symbolic, to show solidarity with those fighting cancer or similar diseases? With the dying? With children, with soldiers? With each other, day to day? With the Earth?

While you're at it, why not invent some new ethical practices out of the blue? Create something completely new!

NOTES

For "Good Morning, Children" I am grateful to Benjamin and Rosamund Zander's book *The Art of Possibility* (Boston: Harvard Business School Press, 2000, p. 164). I have the Heinz dilemma from Kohlberg's article "Stage and Sequence," in D. A. Goslin, editor, *Handbook of Socialization Theory and Research* (Chicago: Rand McNally, 1969, p. 379).

For more on creative problem-solving methods, consult *A 21st Century Ethical Toolbox,* Chapters 15 ("Creative Problem-Solving") and 16 ("Reframing Problems"), or my little book *Creative Problem-Solving in Ethics* (New York/Oxford: Oxford University Press, 2007). On the abortion issue in Japan, see William LaFleur, *Liquid Life: Abortion and Buddhism in Japan* (Princeton, NJ: Princeton University Press, 1994). Further discussion of "dilemma-ism" and the case against it can be found in my book *Toward Better Problems* (Philadelphia, PA: Temple University Press, 1992). For a sampling of the work of Edward de Bono, see his *Lateral Thinking* (New York: Harper and Row, 1970). More creative-thinking tips are available online at www. solutionscreative.com/cpstips.

6

MAKING A DIFFERENCE

~

The aim of ethics is finally to make a difference in the world. For us, coming down to the end of this book, the key thing is to know that we *can* make an ethical difference—and to know how to get started.

CHANGING YOUR LIFE

Ethics may challenge us to rethink what we ourselves do and how we ourselves live, day to day. And, although it is certainly not easy, changing our own lives is one kind of ethical difference that we have a reasonably good chance of making.

Some ethical issues are as close to us as what is on our plates. Many people refuse to eat veal on account of the pure torture (there is no other word) that is often inflicted on calves to produce it. But vegetarians and animal rights activists argue that *most* meat production is on a moral par with veal production. Are they right? What are the implications if so? What are the alternatives?

People who have grown up with the familiar American diet often find it hard to imagine no longer eating meat. Still, say the critics, familiarity alone does not necessarily make anything morally acceptable. It would not be the first time that profound immorality claims a moral pass on the grounds that "everybody does it." Meanwhile, there is a wide range of options, often contending with each other as well. Vegetarian diets exclude animal flesh but may include eggs and dairy products. Vegan diets exclude any product that is produced at the expense of other animals: milk, eggs, honey, leather, and many toiletries and pharmaceuticals. Others argue that eating some animal protein, at least, is vital to health in the long run. Some hold that eating other creatures can be a form of acknowledgment that we too are animals, that we too are parts of nature—that it could even be part of a pro-Earth kind of ethic.

There are also a whole range of other ethical or partly ethical issues involved with eating, from where our food is produced (often locally grown food is ecologically sounder and certainly strengthens local communities—is it therefore also a moral imperative?) to how fast we eat it ("slow food" is a growing movement worldwide, again with moral dimensions you would not expect, such as how we relate to those we eat *with*). Serious and well-informed people take all sides on these questions: there is much to be learned and thought about. New ideas continue to emerge, too.

You may or may not choose to change your diet after you've worked these issues through for yourself. Or you may just need to continue holding the questions, experimenting with your diet without necessarily embracing any final answer. In any case, think about them! The whole issue is a useful reminder that ethics is not just a call to judge some occasional but extreme question that involves only a few of us, but in fact involves *all* of us, all the time, and connects to broader social and political issues as well.

Our sexual lives are another pressing area for ethical reflection. Any ethics of the person insists that sexual love should respond to whole persons—ends in themselves, as everyone from Kant to the Pope puts it, not mere means to pleasure. At the same time, we live in a culture that is sexually demeaning and "objectifying" in many ways, from sexual slang to pornography to sexual harassment. Sometimes it seems that even the most basic sexual respect is difficult, rare, and supposedly not "sexy." We can barely imagine a culture in which it *is* sexy. And yet why not? Really, why not?

The work that we do—our lives as producers, service-people, professionals—affects others, our communities, and the natural world in multiple ways. Are we taking care that the effects are morally supportable? Are they as positive as we can make them? How we spend our income also affects the world. Are we (or how far are we) morally obliged to buy "greener" products? To support more local retailers and producers—the livelihoods of our neighbors and communities? To avoid buying clothes made by virtual slave labor, here and in the rest of the world?

Once again more questions lie beneath these questions in turn. Ethics may ask us to think twice not just about what we buy, but also about the very system in which we relate to others and the world primarily by buying things in the first place. At the very least, shouldn't we buy *less*, live more simply, try to move more important things than shopping into the center of our lives and attention? We say all the time that money is not the only thing that matters, either ethically or any other way—so why, all the same, does money so often seem to be the only thing that matters?

Three Virtues

In meeting challenges like these, I would urge several special virtues.

Attention is one. Simply keep yourself alert to the ethical questions, like these, as they arise in our lives. Don't avoid them, and don't suppose, whatever you may have decided at the moment, that you've answered them once and for all and therefore can just stash them on some mental back shelf and pay no more heed. As this book has been saying from the beginning, ethics invites us to an ongoing mindfulness about how we live in the world. Stay open to the questions. Pay special attention when you find yourself intrigued or unsettled by new information or ideas that come along—those feelings are often a good sign that something needs more thinking.

Explicitness is another relevant virtue. When you think about these issues, keep moral values at the forefront of your attention. Make them explicit. A sexual ethic that truly honors *persons*; a business ethic that returns loyalty to the *community* that makes this business and any business possible; an environmental ethic that cherishes the *whole Earth*—values like these are both guides to your own thinking and rationales you may offer to others.

Once again, though, the point is not to embrace some new dogma and thereafter define yourself (or judge others) by it. Complexity remains. It is not a question of which single moral value is to be your one and only lodestar. You can be explicit about multiple moral values, too. Recognize the ambiguity and changing face of many issues—just be clear about it.

Patience: take manageable steps. These are difficult matters and long-term commitments; you do not have to turn your life upside down overnight. If you become concerned about sexist or racist objectification, for example, just avoiding sexist or racist humor is one good place to start. Work on your habits. Make it a habit never to say something behind someone's back that you would not say to their face. Make it a habit to buy an extra piece of fruit or drink at the grocery store so you have something to give, along with some friendly words, to the homeless person on the corner on the way back. The simplest principle of psychology is that habits like these are established and grow stronger with repetition. They need to be practiced—again and again and again. Yet over time you are building a different character.

Patience also means making changes deliberately and carefully. You do not want to jump into decisions that are not sustainable, however morally satisfying they may feel. I have seen many students decide to give up meat with the best of intentions and goodwill, for instance, only to discover after a month that they cannot, literally, live on bread alone. Of course not! Yet an informed meat-free diet can be easy and extremely healthy, and fellow vegetarians (and cookbooks, grocery stores, restaurants, clubs…) can now be found nearly everywhere. Know your facts and your options.

Finally, be sure to give both yourself and others some credit, even as you continue to be self-aware and self-critical. All of these issues are complicated, and many remain unclear. Meanwhile most of us are already trying to live ethical lives (along with many other things). Already we take care for each other; give generously of our time and resources to help others; teach, doctor, try to raise children well; try to counsel and support those who need help. Ethics just asks us to keep going, still more mindfully and rigorously (and perchance, still more constructively and creatively) in the same directions—and also, just as important, each in our own ways and our own good time.

CHANGING THE WORLD

Ethics of course also enters the public sphere. We may seek to make larger changes in how our society operates or in the prevailing moral understandings and relation ships. Here again, a brief look at ways and means may be helpful.

The Power of One

There are many quiet and devoted ways to change the world one small step at a time. There are also some less quiet ways—and certain people, in particular, who may inspire even those of us who do not follow in their rather bigger footsteps.

Ethical individuals can and do change the world! Take Nelson Mandela, South African, who spent his life fighting apartheid and the governments that enforced it and served twenty-seven years in prison, often in solitary confinement or at hard labor, for that fight. He came out of that prison still committed to creating—in his famous words from the dock as he was being hauled off to jail—"a democratic and free society in which all persons live together in harmony and with equal opportunities." In 1994, as blacks attained the right to vote for the first time, the previously banned African National Congress swept to power and Mandela became the first black president of South Africa.

Muhammed Yunus, Bangladeshi banker, is the creator of "micro-credit"—a good example of making a difference by creative thinking. Yunus came to realize that even very small loans to otherwise destitute village craftspeople can free those people from middlemen and make them canny and effective entrepreneurs. Scaffolded by support groups but with no collateral requirement and no repayment date, his loans are still repaid sooner and at a higher rate than those from most banks—out of, basically, *gratitude*. His Grameen Bank is now the largest rural bank in Bangladesh, with millions of borrowers and spinoffs the world over, including more than 500 in the United States.

Anita Roddick is an English entrepreneur who started the Body Shop, now a major multinational corporation, standing from the beginning for fair trade, environmental responsibility, and the empowerment of women, and insistently educating anyone who comes in her stores about those issues. For her company, ethics actually is a *selling point*, not just a way of staying ahead of the law, or even just of doing their part. Roddick pushed her company always to do *more* than their part, indeed to do as much as they possibly could do: pioneering corporate social and environmental audits and Community Trade campaigns, for example, and dealing transparently and directly with indigenous producers and collectives.

World-changers like these are highly honored: they are presidents, international bankers, a CEO. But they started in ordinary places. Roddick, for example, started out just wanting to set up a little shop for her friends to keep her family going in tight financial times (and at first only attracted the attention of a nearby undertaker, who objected to the name). But her ethical insight was that beauty products have real people's lives and real places behind them, which we need to recognize and protect. Why would we choose to rub the products of exploitation and destruction into our very skins? Her customers made the connection—and kept coming back.

Yunus, university-trained abroad, came home to find his country's economy in a shambles and quickly realized that his training was useless to help him understand and respond to it. He took to the streets, dragging his unwilling students along, until he found himself listening to destitute village craftspeople. When he saw an opportunity in what they told him, he pulled out his own wallet. "The bankers laughed at him, insisting that the poor are not 'creditworthy', [but] Yunus answered, 'How do you know they are not creditworthy, if you've never tried? Perhaps it is the banks that are not people-worthy?'" So he created his own.

In short, Roddick and Yunnus started small, with individual acts of perceptiveness, kindness, initiative. It is not somehow only extraordinary people who change the world. It is more as though ordinary people *become* extraordinary *through* changing the world.

There are plenty of these extra/ordinary people right around us. Right in my community and among people I know personally, there are artists who have created arts and crafts festivals to revitalize their neighborhoods. There are hospice workers and advocates and volunteers. There are specialists in socially responsible investments and in counseling desperate and unready new mothers. There are volunteer coaches, youth group leaders, nature guides. There is the creator of a new organization to promote long-term adaptive thinking about climate change. At my university, students are working to bring locally grown and organic food into the university cafeterias, supporting local growers and introducing fellow students to totally new ways to eat. Professors and students and staff are building homes with Habitat for Humanity, tutoring needy school kids, staffing local social services and health organizations and prison ministries, and much more.

All of this is happening right now, as I have said, and in my own experience—one person's small world. Your world, I am sure, has similar sorts of openings and possibilities. At my school, for example, each of the projects just mentioned began with one or two students or staff-people speaking out or stepping up to try to make an ethical difference. Next time, why not *you*?

"Realism"—and Beyond

"You can't change the world!"—I imagine you have heard that a few thousand times, maybe especially when you get optimistic and energetic about working for some ethical transformation. The examples I have just given may help to persuade you that moral change is possible after all, although it is certainly not easy or without criticism or controversy. But there is another and more philosophical argument as well.

People and situations always have hidden possibilities. Beware of the self-satisfied "realism" that looks at the world as it is (or anyway *seems,* to some people) and imagines that the world that we know to be the only world that is possible. Muhammad Yunus puts it well:

> Poverty covers people in a thick crust and makes the poor appear stupid and without initiative. Yet if you give them credit, they will slowly come back to life. Even those who seemingly have no conceptual thought, no ability to think of yesterday or tomorrow, are in fact quite intelligent and expert at the art of survival. Credit is the key that unlocks their humanity.

The thought here is a deep one. Yunus proposes that everyone has the ingenuity to lift themselves out of poverty—but we aren't going to *see* that ingenuity, he says, until it is invited to show itself. In general, the world may well look "stuck," unchangeable, until someone or something acts to create a new kind of opening. The opening has to come *first*, in short. We have to "give some credit"—a pretty pun, in his case. *Then* we can see some change. Ethics, so understood, asks us to take some risks. Remember your moral vision!

Likewise, Nelson Mandela actually imagined that South Africans could forgive the apartheid regime for the decades of oppression it fostered, and blacks and whites could attempt to go on together. It certainly didn't look that way when majority rule first loomed—the world expected a bloodbath—yet the kind of forward-looking forgiveness he himself modeled, even in the face of the strongest of incitements to hatred and revenge (for everyone, black and white alike, knew Mandela's story), prevailed in the end. He was right—and his own example and confidence helped to make it so.

So don't be deterred by the "realists" who look at the present situation and see no hope. Often we have only the

barest idea of what is really possible. "Realism" may only
be an excuse for resignation, or lack of imagination, or
unwillingness to try. The realists may actually be right in a
way: maybe there really is no hope in the present situation.
Your response might be that therefore we need to *change
the situation.*

Ways and Means

There are many ways to try to change the world. Different
people bring different abilities, take different tacks, act for
different reasons. Mandela brought his courage and eloquence and tenacity. Roddick brought a moral persistence
and a "why not?" attitude to the world of business. Yunus
brought his willingness to listen, to trust, and ultimately
his ability to invent a whole new form of banking. Rosa
Parks, whose refusal to give up her bus seat to a white man
sparked the Montgomery Bus Boycott that helped to bring
down racial segregation in America, simply was tired—
"tired of giving in."

And you? You, too, may bring courage or persistence or
creativity or other virtues, maybe special to you, to opportunities that are also distinctive and changing. Or maybe
you, too, are just "tired of giving in." Look to your own situation and setting to see what might be done. Maybe you
want to call your college or university to stop selling goods
produced in sweatshops or to live up to higher standards
of environmental sustainability. Causes like these call for
their own kinds of engagement. Ecological responsibility
lends itself especially well to modeling: showing others
how it can be done by doing it, joyfully and effectively,
yourself. Both of these issues, and many others like them,
also call for more *education,* and you are (let's suppose)

a student at an educational institution, so ... how about organizing a teach-in or some other dramatic or inviting way to educate others?

During your college years, one of your most significant ethical choices may be that career path you choose and how you choose to practice that career. Ask yourself, early on, what careers you could practice, given your interests and abilities, that would help make the world a better place. Or, if you are already embarked on a career path—education, medicine, the military, the arts, business, the ministry, community organizing...—ask how can you bring ethics, or more ethics, to it. Can you take up your chosen work more creatively, can you find more person-affirming, social-good–producing, virtuous ways to practice it?

In the long run, how might you make yourself a model for others? How could you, like Anita Roddick, make fairness to others and environmental responsibility into selling-points, keys to the very attraction, of your business or profession? What's the next step—and the step after that? One of your opportunities as a young person, just setting out, is flexibility. Make the most of it!

Once again, keep the key moral values explicit. Mandela and Parks, in their different ways, stood up for racial equality. Yunus's micro-credit explicitly serves economic justice. Help run a business and you get a sense of what it means to meet a payroll, sustain other people's livelihoods, organize a common effort to exacting standards. Build a house with Habitat for Humanity and you get a glimpse of a world in which decent housing is a community responsibility rather than the indulgence of a bank. Crucial to the moral effectiveness of all of these people and organizations is that they keep their essential values clear and upfront—for themselves but also, persistently, for others as well, sometimes especially for those who sometimes do not really want to hear them.

Again, too, do not just mention such moral values in a rhetorical and passing way and then quickly move on to practical measures. Take the time and care to *explain* why you care about these values, and in a way that invites others to join you—to recognize how important these values are, or should be, to them too. Remember that you are not just trying to make a practical change but also a moral change: to shift the visibility and priority of certain values themselves.

And of course patience, and an openness to complexity and ambiguity, are as essential here as in making other kinds of change. Acknowledge that there are other values in play. It is not as though you have the whole story to yourself, although you may well have some piece that needs a lot more attention. Listen to your critics, for they have things to teach you as well. Don't imagine that everything, or even much of anything, is going to change overnight. On the other hand, again, remember that much more is possible than we often think. Just move ahead as best you can, and let things work out as they will.

MAKING CHANGE TOGETHER

Everywhere communities are doing ethical work. Every city has marches to raise money to stock food banks or help cure diabetes. Others work toward downtown revitalization—for when inner cities are cut off and impoverished, the whole community is affected, and the walls of fear and denial begin to rise. "Communities in the Schools" programs aim to keep kids in school through adult mentoring.

WRITING TO MAKE A DIFFERENCE

One way to make an ethical difference is through *writing*. As a student, in fact, you may be in an especially good position to do so—for writing need not simply be an academic exercise, even in school. Here are some guidelines for *writing to make a difference*.

Know Your Goal

First of all, know what kind of difference you want to make. There are many possibilities. Maybe some moral issue or ethical theory intrigues you and you want to find out more. Your goal then is just to *explore the issue*. Or your goal may be to *witness*: to share some of what you have experienced personally about a moral issue— but without closing it down or closing out others' perhaps quite different experiences. Your goal may be to *get unstuck*: to help to get a group or a community past some of the sticking points in a moral debate as it stands. Or you may need, or be required, to *make a case*: to argue for one view on an issue for yourself or others.

All of these goals are different, and there are other possible goals too. Which is yours? For a class assignment, if you are not sure whether a particular goal is appropriate, be sure to ask!

Work Explicitly from Moral Values

A recent ethics class of mine wanted to raise campus awareness of the need to recycle. The first task was to lay it out as a moral vision: to clearly state the values in play and then spell them out and connect them to other values.

One student drafted a vision statement, a small committee reworked it, and then the whole class helped give it final shape. The final statement began with an overview:

> Our actions impact the whole planet in ways that can imperil the health of the entire ecological system as well as our own well-being and even survival. As we enter the ecological age, more awareness of our effects and dependence on nature is crucial.

Then it tied in other values—painting on a large canvas indeed:

> While our culture has exalted independence and individualism above all else ... truly we need to view individualism in its proper context, as one of *many* values we hold dear. [We propose] a more comprehensive and nuanced view of as individuals—individuals who also value and respect the larger communities of which we are members.

We spoke of the human community across time—of the need for "trans-generational justice"—as well, and ended by invoking a deep reverence and respect for nature itself.

> Regardless of whether one believes in divine creation, when we reflect on the sequence of events that led to our existence at this place and time on Earth, we find ourselves with a sense of wonder and awe at the miracle of simply being, a miracle inextricably linked to and sustained by the whole encompassing environment... . It is this insight—the recognition of the sanctity of the environment within which we live—that allows us to temper individualism ... with the virtues of moderation, fairness, and respect that lie at the heart of [our] project.

Seldom have I seen recycling explained with such eloquence or depth or broad-based appeal! It is not just some annoying new chore, but part of a movement toward a new ethical relation to the Earth itself. When the class then went on to various kinds of action—researching and promoting the composting of cafeteria food wastes, for example, and modeling a "zero-waste" campus event—the whole campus community could clearly see how they fit into a very big moral picture.

Write unto Others as You Would Have Them Write unto You

Show your ethics in how you yourself write. Do not be dismissive of other people or of moral issues or problems that they take seriously.

Not that you have to agree with them—but don't brush them aside as not even worth thinking about. Use your writing to connect, not disconnect. Imagine you are sitting face to face with someone you respect but who holds a different and maybe even opposite view on the specific question at issue. *Now* respond to their arguments and concerns.

Write with a visible openness to the diversity of ethical views and complexity of issues as well. On flashpoint issues especially, try not to inflame passions further. Bring people together. Can your writing make new allies, even of those who hold different views? Can it serve moral community, rather than diminish it?

Go Public

Clearly identify your audience, write with that audience in mind, and then share your writing with that audience. To witness or make a case, you might compose a letter to the editor of your school or city paper. If you're more ambitious, write something longer and more worked out. Many publications welcome submissions for guest editorials. The fate of your letter or editorial (whether it gets published, what reactions it provokes or inspires, etc.) will teach you a lot about how to write a more effective one next time. And there is no better way to remind yourself that you need to have something thoughtful, new, and well worked out to say if you are going to join a public dialogue on an issue that matters.

Whatever kind of writing you do, at least share your results with your classmates. Or join with them to do some of the writing together. Consider setting up a class forum on some pressing issues. Write up explanatory materials. Open it to your university and to your larger community as well. My classes have launched teach-ins, worked with student government committees and university administrators to make changes on campus, put up idea boards and started on-line groups to encourage deeper and more creative ethical thinking on specific issues and opportunities. To interact with a larger audience, take part in community meetings and campaigns and submit your write-ups to online forums on ethical and social issues.

You can help in the libraries; you can tutor kids in math or English or history; you can help soldiers serving abroad with support for their families back home; you can build houses with Habitat for Humanity, usually alongside the people who will be living in them ("sweat equity" indeed), joining other volunteers and groups from across the community. The Community-Supported Agriculture movement aims to preserve rural open space, water quality, and small farms along with the communities that go with them. People buy the produce directly, so they know where it comes from. Sometimes they help work the farms themselves.

There are so many voluntary organizations with an ethical slant that a quick Web search turns up over three hundred just in my own area: Americorps Youth Mentoring, Amnesty International, Child Abuse and Family Violence Prevention, Doctors Without Borders, Fair Housing Advocacy, groups to fight blindness, Guardian Ad Litem programs, Hospice, the Humane Society, Keep America Beautiful, Make-A-Wish, Meals on Wheels, Mothers Against Drunk Driving, groups to limit kids' exposure to TV, Refugee Aid, Relay for Life (anti-cancer), road clean-ups, StandUp for Kids (helping homeless and street kids), Student Literacy Coalition, Stop Hunger Now, Rails-to-Trails Conservancies, urban gardening organizations ("working together to create green areas of neighborhood pride and enjoyment"), the World Library Partnership ("advocates for sustainable, community-based libraries in developing areas of the world"), the World Wildlife Fund ... until finally the alphabet runs out.

Notice also that a wide of approaches are involved. Some kinds of change are immediate and direct, like responding to an emergency or making a drastic change in policy. Others are slower and work more in the background, like trying to keep more kids in school (preventing a whole range of thornier problems down the road) or preserving locally-owned media (enabling more diverse and locally-empowered discussion of *other* issues). Likewise different kinds of change may call for very different strategies, sometimes even on the same issue. Direct-action strategies coexist readily with longer-term structural change goals.

Join some of this work. Find somewhere you are needed and can make a real contribution. Again, your task is to find a good fit for *you*: for your resources, your skills, and what you see as the most pressing demands of the moment. Enlist with like-minded others and put your shoulders to the wheel.

Actually, it is quite likely that you belong to change-making communities already—you may just need to embrace them as such. If you belong to a religious congregation, for example, explore what kinds of social or community work your congregation is already involved with. Is more help needed? Where is there potential to broaden the work?

At your job—say in a business or corporation—ask the same kinds of questions. How can the business become a force, or still more of a force, for ethical change? How can you help mobilize that force? Look at the quality of your company's products; look at your company's overall effects on the community and the environment; look at the nature of relationships within the company itself. What are the best next steps?

If you are a student, consider that simply being a student gives you a natural solidarity with other students. Students are organizing across campuses, across the country, even across the world. Despite how it may sometimes feel, students have power precisely *as students*. Students stand in the forefront of the movement against sweatshops, for example, because universities are among the prime customers for products made in sweatshops: clothes stamped with university logos. Students have leverage at their own institutions, and universities, being large singe-order customers, have leverage over suppliers.

Be ready to help out in whatever way you can. But remember also that, having studied ethics a little more than others may have, you may bring some distinctive skills to this work. You could be the one, for instance, who pushes your organization or community toward more creative ethical thinking. We have seen that there are often entirely unexpected and inspiring ways to bring ethical values into action. One "out of the box" solution to the problem of sweatshops, for example, is for universities to start producing their *own* clothes, using local materials and know-how as well, thereby promoting (and why not also teaching?) local crafts and sustainability as well. You could be the one to seek and find options like these. Others, not so trained or encouraged, may not. Think Big!

Finally, once again, there is the task of making moral values more explicit and connected. Your organization may have an ethical mission statement already. Your community may already know what ethical values it needs to speak for. Then again, it seldom hurts to be more explicit about the key values—and oftentimes, at least in my experience, organizations and communities tend to move all too quickly past the ethical basics to concentrate on immediate practical issues.

Some organizations already have quite extraordinary ethical aspirations. Did you know that Toyota officially aspires to produce cars that never crash and that clean up the environment as they drive? Our own country is still working on securing the rights of life, liberty, and the pursuit of happiness for all. Day to day—as citizens, at work, as members of multiple communities—we need to remember these things. We need to re-invoke and re-embrace the visions.

Other times, communities need their visions made more explicit, the aspirations clearly stated—and then, perhaps, raised. And *you* have some of the concepts and skills, now, to help to do so: to call your organization or community more clearly and explicitly back to its fundamental ethical commitments. And then, at the same time... perhaps also to another step forward.

FOR PRACTICE

Review

Summarize and review the main points of this chapter. What kinds of challenges might ethical thinking pose to how we live our daily lives? How do we go about taking up and thinking through these challenges? How does ethics engage people to change the world—and again, how can you join the work? How do you "write to change the world"? And how might we do all of this *together*?

Reframing Your Options

Make a list of careers—you might even compile a list of the career aspirations of the students in your class—and brainstorm less and more ethical ways of practicing each of them. What are more socially and environmentally responsible ways of practicing medicine or building houses or raising children or cooking in a restaurant? How to better serve the greater happiness, respect persons, build virtue? Consider your real needs: how much of an income do you really need to live the way you find most appealing and most morally appropriate?

Right now perhaps your "career" is in school. So ask: are there less and more ethical ways of being a student? Again brainstorm some possibilities together. You might go on to pick one or two changes to try to make right now. Can you be more supportive of each other as learners? Can you be more respectful of your learning community's resources? Can your learning community welcome others not usually included—and as equals, people with something to offer, not just as charity cases? Can you treat the people or communities you study, say in psychology and the social sciences, as real people and not just as objects to be generalized about? And: since many kinds of generosity sustain nearly every educational institution (from government support to alumni donations to teachers and staff who give far more than expected), what are some ways you as students might give back?

Here is another possible thought-experiment. Imagine that your education has been offered to you totally free on one condition: that afterward, for, say, five years, you are required to find an imaginative and adventurous way to make the world a morally better place. You are expressly forbidden to get a standard job or "settle down." Work out some ideas about what your alternative work/life could be. Then find three actual, existing job openings or programs that are actually hiring or looking for people to do something like this work—conceivably someone just like you. Make contact with at least one. Now what?

Change Projects

Commit yourself as a class to a project of ethical change. Expect it to be a learning experience about basic values as well as the nitty-gritty of getting change moving. Work at constructive dialogue both between yourselves and with others. Get your facts straight. Speak and act mindfully. Use your creativity and vision. Be ambitious—reach farther than your realists think you can go—but, of course, choose a project you have at least some chance to carry through in the time you have together.

Note that this work may be quite different than "service" or "service-learning." Service is helping: dealing with immediate need by offering aid and succor. Change-making more likely addresses the causes of need themselves and/or promotes changes that offer all of us opportunities for ethical transformation and better understanding.

I have described some my own students' environmental work. Lately they have also initiated such projects as making our school more connected and responsive on issues of race—working to make race issues more prominent and consistent in the curriculum and forging links between the university and communities of color right next door. Another group constructed a website for local teens to get them sex-education information they were being denied in their own schools, along with local resources and help designed to promote sexual self-possession and self-determination. Then they handed off the site to local high-schoolers themselves. My most recent class entered into partnership with a local homeless shelter, building new bed-frames for the shelter alongside some of the residents, while also arranging for lightly used mattresses from university dorms to be delivered to the shelter at the end of the school year to replace the ragged collection of mattresses they currently use. We also facilitated long-term partnerships between campus organizations and the shelter and local families on the edge.

On the Web, you can search for local volunteer opportunities with just the name of your city or area and a simple keyword like "volunteer." Or begin with an issue or problem and survey the organizations already at work on it. Look for the unexplored and undeveloped possibilities that might have the greatest new promise. Much more is happening—and much more is possible—than we usually think. Find an opening and embrace the work. And of course, good luck!

NOTES

The lines cited in the text about Muhammed Yunus come from Alan Jolis's "The Good Banker," *The Independent on Sunday Supplement* (London), May 5, 1996, and can be found online, along with much other useful information, at http://www. grameen-info.org/. The values statement cited in the box on "Writing to Make a Difference" was drafted by a small student group with input from the whole class. The primary author was Jack McMackin. For more on this project, visit http://org.elon. edu/lightenup/.

Please consult *A 21st Century Ethical Toolbox* for three full chapters (Part IV, "Making a Difference") on the themes of this one, including many more extended examples of people and organizations making inspiring and suggestive kinds of change, along with much more advice and useful links as well.